INSPIRATION
TO INK

The Big Picture of How We Got the Bible

MIKE WILSON

ISBN-13: 978-0-89098-853-6

Interior design, typesetting and cover by Hinds Design (www.HindsDesign.com).
Cover images: 1572 Bishops' Bible, © *David Posey*

Wilson, Mike.
  Inspiration To Ink: The Big Picture of How We Got the Bible / Mike Wilson.

I dedicate this book, and any good it happens to accomplish, to the great God and Father of our Lord Jesus Christ, the only true and living God, who has blessed me beyond my wildest imaginations. I pray that you allow him to do the same for you.

CONTENTS

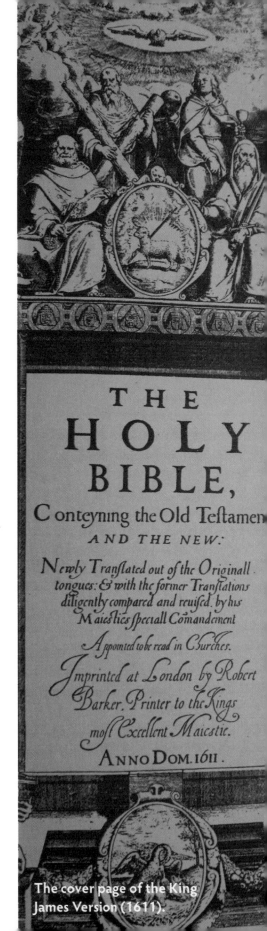

The cover page of the King James Version (1611).

ENDORSEMENTS

Mike Wilson has become one of the most proficient and articulate writers of his generation. In this, his latest book, *Inspiration To Ink: The Big Picture of How We Got The Bible*, he skillfully addresses two of the most prevalent questions of the past century: "How did we get the Bible?" and "Can we trust it to be the inspired word of God?" As a research scientist with more than 40 years of experience, I can attest that Mike's research efforts are thorough and of the highest quality. This book should be in every Christian's private library as well as in all church libraries.

Mike has wisely divided the book into 13 lessons, so it will fit nicely into the Bible class colloquium using the quarter system. All Christians can benefit from reading/studying this book. In particular, teenagers and young people, having studied the material in this book, will be well-suited to deal with questions about the authenticity of the Bible that arise from agnostics, skeptics, etc. throughout their life time.
  —**Dr. David M. Cooper**, Retired Research Scientist at
  NASA Ames Research Center, Moffett Field, California

Curious: Every serious God-follower and Christ-believer has, at some point, grappled with the issue of the reliability and accuracy of the biblical text. *Intimidated:* The mountains of technical material and unfamiliar verbiage in support of the Scriptures are often daunting to those without an academic, theological background. *Thankful:* Serious students should be grateful for the masterful work Mike Wilson has done in resolving those two issues.

Inspiration To Ink: The Big Picture of How We Got the Bible is a serious presentation of the external scholarly and internal biblical materials that substantiate the trustworthiness of the text (supplemented by several lists of 'Helpful Resources' that are just what the name implies). And it presents those materials in a way that is both understandable and relevant (supplemented by "Questions" at the end of each chapter that are applicable, thought-provoking inquiries designed to highlight the practical nature of the text).

I'm happy to recommend this volume as a valuable addition to the library of every serious Bible student.

—**Don Truex**, Temple Terrace Church of Christ, Temple Terrace, Florida; evangelist and elder

Mike Wilson's *Inspiration to Ink: The Big Picture of How We Got the Bible* is a valuable study for anyone wishing to explore the rich history of God's written Word, from its ancient documents to its translation into the English language. He has not only simplified centuries of history regarding the Bible itself, but he has effectively dispelled many of the accusations offered by those who have been critical of the accuracy of the biblical text. The work is scholarly and the photographs are captivating. You will be glad you went through this study!

—**Brent Willey**, Evangelist and elder, Los Osos Church of Christ, Los Osos, California

For Mike, this work has been a labor of love. He has spent so much of his time and personal resources to bring the history of the Bible to life. Over 100 high-quality images grace the pages of this new workbook on the history of the Bible, revealing his passion for this subject. Mike has performed meticulous research and crafted his words carefully because he wanted to make the presentation as simple and effective as possible.

—**Marc Hinds**, author of *The Big Picture: A Guide to Learning the Bible's Story* and *Amazed By Jesus*

PHOTO CREDITS

The tetragrammaton, YHWH (Yahweh, the LORD) in a Geneva Bible, 1607

INTRODUCTION

A couple of years ago, I began to collect old Bibles. In fact, it's not a stretch to say, as I sometimes joke, that I sold a house in California and bought some books. Antique Bibles are works of art. The rarer and more ancient they are, the better the "investment." As one dealer says, like California real estate, there is a finite amount to sell. After all, they aren't making any more of them. A Tyndale Bible can go for $500,000 (or more), and first edition copies of the King James Version start at about $100,000. I have much more limited tastes (along with a limited budget to match), but I have been blessed to collect some notable facsimiles, reprints, and a few museum-quality original editions of ancient Bibles.

More importantly, biblical manuscripts, medieval documents, and early English Bibles tell a story. As one looks at each historical stage, a powerful case begins to develop about the integrity of the transmission process. The cast of characters includes a faithful God, an amazing Lord who said the most powerful things that anyone ever uttered, and a Holy Spirit who guided prophets and apostles to record the message. It also involves angels and men—holy men who in many cases paid a heavy personal price to make possible the widespread access to the Bible that we sometimes take for granted.

I wanted to write this book for common people, not professional scholars. I designed it either as 13 chapters for personal study, or 13 lessons for group and church classes. Omitted are certain technical issues of textual criticism that sometimes become a "turn off." Instead the focus is on issues that should resonate with every earnest believer. To make this material relevant, and even fun, many full-color photographs are included in the pages to follow.

Rogier van der Weyden,
The Magdalen Reading

I want to thank David Posey and Kambiz Rahmani for taking many of the photos, and to Marc Hinds for his tireless and meticulous design work. My wife, Andrea, is a German with an eye for detail. She introduced me to many historical sites and museums in her native Europe that impacted my appreciation of key events. She also proofread the text and offered valuable suggestions.

As I write, we have plans to launch a one-day museum exhibit on the transmission history of the Bible, with different local church members working each station. After receiving firsthand exposure to manuscripts, replicas, and original documents and books, visitors will walk away with a greater awareness of the integrity of the Bible. Many of them will also be given a copy of this book.

We live in an age in which many people take unfair shots at the Bible. As a matter of fact, the case for the integrity of God's Word has never been stronger. We just need to familiarize ourselves with the most relevant details and articulate the case to others. With that noble goal in mind, I affectionately commit this little work into the hands of friends and family members, and to others "afar off " who may benefit from a greater appreciation of the world's greatest Book!

Geneva Bible, 1607

LESSON 1
God Spoke to Man

The Message of the Bible

The Bible claims to be a message from God to mankind. The first book in the Bible, Genesis, begins with the words, "In the beginning, God…" The prophets regularly open their discourses with the formula, "Thus says the LORD…" Jesus claimed,

> "My teaching is not mine, but his who sent me. If anyone's will is to do God's will, he will know whether the teaching is from God or whether I am speaking on my own authority" (John 7:16–17).

The apostle Paul declared,

> And we also thank God constantly for this, that when you received the word of God, which you heard from us, you accepted it not as the word of men but as what it really is, the word of God, which is at work in you believers (1 Thess 2:13).

The implicit authority of the Bible is tied to its claim of supernatural origin.

The Process of Communication

According to the Scriptures, God revealed his message to certain chosen individuals during carefully timed moments of biblical history. Hebrews 1:1–2 says,

> Long ago, at many times and in many ways, God spoke to our fathers by the prophets, but in these last days he has spoken to us by his Son…

How did God convey his will "at many times and in many ways"? The message was communicated in bits and pieces, not in its entirety. Through dreams, visions, theophanies, angels, and other means, "God spoke by the mouth of his holy prophets long ago" (Acts 3:21).

This resulted in a variety of channels of communication. Among other forms of transmission, the Bible's human messengers utilized law codes, historical reports, sermons, prophetic oracles, songs, play acting, epistles, poems, proverbs, parables, legal briefs, debates, captivating stories, outbursts of praise, curse formulas, covenants, royal decrees, genealogical records, funeral dirges, wild apocalyptic images, and heartfelt prayers. God is determined to get our attention, one way or another.

Cumulative Revelation

The Bible was revealed in stages. It is a book that required at least 40 commissioned human writers, on three continents, over 1,500 years to complete. There are two major sections, called the Old Testament, written mostly in Hebrew, and the New Testament (or Covenant), written in Greek. As the Bible is a multi-volume work, there are 39 "books" in the Old Testament, and 27 in the New Covenant. These books span three great dispensations of time: the Patriarchal age, the Mosaic period, and the New Testament Church.

Part of the reason for cumulative revelation over time had to do with preparing the world incrementally to receive the full message. The story of the Bible is that of a hands-on God intervening

through history to save a lost world. Prophecies, sometimes made hundreds of years in advance, anticipate later developments. The entire Old Testament is best seen as a preparation for the New Testament.

> But when the fullness of time had come, God sent forth his Son, born of woman, born under the law (Gal 4:4).

Complete

God intended the Bible to be the final authority, or the *go-to source*, for "all things that pertain to life and godliness" (2 Pet 1:3). One of the foundational statements in Scripture on the matter is this one from the apostle Paul:

> All Scripture is breathed out by God and profitable for teaching, for reproof, for correction, and for training in righteousness, that the man of God may be complete, equipped for every good work (2 Tim 3:16–17).

We must believe that at the outset of the process is a God who took initiative to reveal his Word and to safeguard the process that would ultimately make it accessible to people far and wide. The apostle Peter says,

> Knowing this first of all, that no prophecy of Scripture comes from someone's own interpretation. For no prophecy was ever produced by the will of man, but men spoke from God as they were carried along by the Holy Spirit (2 Pet 1:20–21).

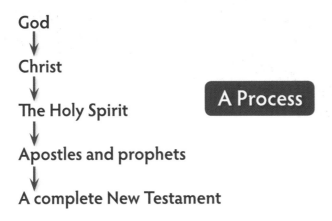

God
↓
Christ
↓
The Holy Spirit   A Process
↓
Apostles and prophets
↓
A complete New Testament

What was true of the Old Testament prophets is also true of the New Testament. There is ultimately a carefully delegated chain of command at work:

God the Father speaks through his Son, Jesus Christ (John 12:48–50; Matt 17:5). Jesus in turn sends the Holy Spirit (John 14:26; 15:26; 16:12–13). The Holy Spirit would reveal the New Covenant through "holy apostles and prophets" (Eph 3:3–5). The apostles and prophets taught the revealed message by "spoken word" or written "letter" (2 Thess 2:15). The subsequent message is called

- ► the "command of the Lord" (1 Cor 14:37);
- ► "the word of God" (1 Thess 2:13); and
- ► "the faith once for all delivered to the saints" (Jude 3).

As one can see from reading each of the passages above, no deviations were allowed at any stage of the process.

My mother's Bible, bequeathed to me at her death. It has been said that when you see a Bible falling apart at the seams, you can be fairly certain that its owner is well put together.

Bonus Material—
Evidence for Divine Revelation

The acceptance of the divine origin of the Bible's message is not taken for granted. The work of prophets and apostles was "confirmed" to contemporary people of God by predictive prophecies, miraculous signs, and eyewitness testimony. God wanted to demonstrate the legitimacy of his chosen messengers through objective, verifiable means, so that people could have confidence in the message (John 20:30–31; 2 Pet 1:16–22; Heb 2:3–4).

As the message was being revealed, whenever there was a direct conflict between the true messengers of God and false spokesmen, powerful and amazing demonstrations vindicated those who spoke the truth over the counterfeit practitioners (Gen 41; Ex 7:8–12; 8:19; 1 Kings 18; Jer 28; Dan 2; Acts 13:6–12). Fake revelations were thereby exposed for what they really were.

Questions

1. State some solid reasons why you believe that the Bible is the Word of God.

2. Many people put false confidence in subjective feelings about what they feel God wants them to believe. This is something the Bible explicitly warns us against (Prov 3:5; 14:12; Jer 10:23). What advantages does the process outlined in this lesson have above *personal feelings* about the will of God?

3. "That's not how I would have done it!" This is perhaps a typical thought when people confront the Bible for the first time. After all, God revealed this message over 1,500 years, through at least 40 human messengers, in two major covenants. Read Isa 55:8–9. Are there some advantages in revealing the Bible in so many stages, through so many chosen people?

4. The Bible makes some claims that are rather outrageous… unless they happen to be true. What are some lines of evidence in the case for legitimacy?

Helpful References

J. W. McGarvey (1829–1911), *Evidences of Christianity*. 1891.

James Orr (1844–1913), *Revelation and Inspiration.*
Charles Scribner's Sons, 1910.

Code of Hammurabi, Pergamon Museum, Berlin. This is an ancient law code that invites comparisons to the Law of Moses in the Bible.

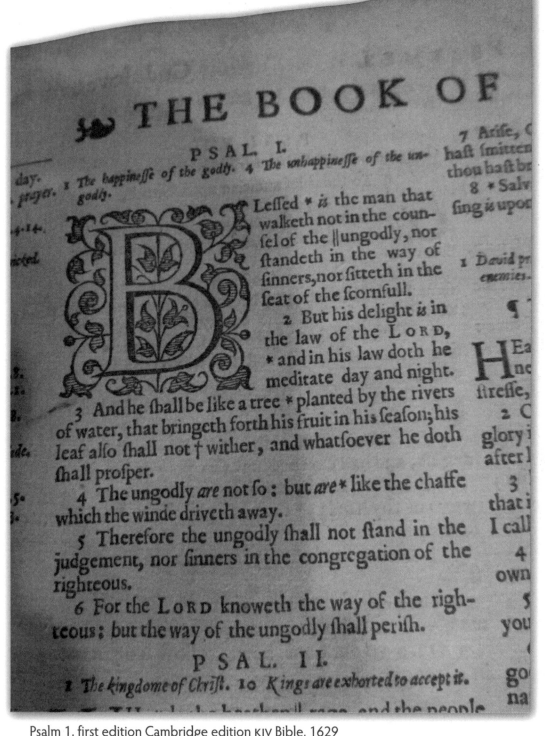

THE BOOK OF

PSAL. I.

1 The happinesse of the godly. 4 The unhappinesse of the ungodly.

Blessed * *is* the man that walketh not in the counsel of the ||ungodly, nor standeth in the way of sinners, nor sitteth in the seat of the scornfull.

2 But his delight *is* in the law of the LORD, * and in his law doth he meditate day and night.

3 And he shall be like a tree * planted by the rivers of water, that bringeth forth his fruit in his season; his leaf also shall not † wither, and whatsoever he doth shall prosper.

4 The ungodly *are* not so : but *are* * like the chaffe which the winde driveth away.

5 Therefore the ungodly shall not stand in the judgement, nor sinners in the congregation of the righteous.

6 For the LORD knoweth the way of the righteous: but the way of the ungodly shall perish.

PSAL. II.

1 The kingdome of Christ. 10 Kings are exhorted to accept it.

Psalm 1, first edition Cambridge edition KJV Bible, 1629

LESSON 2
Organizing the Message

From Oral Transmission to Writing

There is a popular "fake narrative" floating around. Critics assume that the Bible is a hodgepodge of myths and legends, and that the "word of mouth" transmission of the episodes assures that the message was hopelessly garbled over time. Nothing could be further from the truth.

There are three false assumptions in this line of reasoning.

First, even in cases where oral transmission of events occurred, not enough credit is given to ancient memory skills. In a pre-mass media society, ancient people valued extensive memorization of their repository of key traditions that were handed down from generation to generation. As several studies have suggested, the ancients were much more adept at restating exact details than moderns, whose memory muscles tend to go dormant as they rely more on print and technological crutches.

Second, there is too little regard for the divine power in preserving a message or in guiding the process. The help of the Holy Spirit is clearly a factor in the preservation of biblical events.

Third, the time lag between the events themselves and the written recording of those events was much shorter than is sometimes assumed—often in the lifetime of the eyewitnesses themselves.

Luke and Mark, painted wood cover (7th century) of the Codex Washingtonianus (c. A.D. 400)

As a message rooted in historical events, the Bible is the by-product of reports by those who were "chosen by God as witnesses" (Acts 10:41). Confidence in what really happened is not helped by unreliable reports, so God chose "holy apostles and prophets" (Eph 3:5), i.e. people of impeccable character, integrity, motives, and honesty. Consequently, many of the accounts convey a first-hand, "we were there!" impression (Acts 2:32; 5:32; 2 Pet 1:16ff.; 1 John 1:1–4). As a case study that is representative of much broader material, we start with the reports of the most important person in the Bible—Jesus.

Case Study: How the Gospels Came into Being

The three synoptic Gospels of Matthew, Mark, and Luke, in some sections, bear a striking resemblance to one another, with an almost word-for-word correspondence. In other sections, there is independence in both content and form, leading to charges of apparent contradiction. The explanation for this curious mixture of similarity and diversity, according to many critics, lies in partial copying, combined with an almost freelance creativity on the part of those who produced the documents. This standard explanation, regurgitated almost mindlessly in certain "academic" circles, leaves much to be desired. Moreover, it implies that Matthew, Mark, and Luke were less than honorable in their handling of information.

A much better explanation can be deduced from a careful reading of the New Testament itself. From the earliest days of the church, disciples continued steadfastly in "the apostles' teaching" (Acts 2:42). Under the apostles' tutelage, a careful distinction was maintained between "cleverly devised tales" and authentic remembrances verified by eyewitness testimony (2 Pet 1:16; Acts 5:32; 1 John 1:1–3). A big part of the "ministry of the word" for the apostles was the permanent record of the life of Christ, which they have faithfully recorded for all posterity. It is precisely these documented remembrances that Luke has in mind when he says that "eyewitnesses and servants of the word have handed them down to us" (Luke 1:2). There were likely at least four stages in the transmission of the life of Christ.

opposite page
Matthew's Gospel, Harper Illuminated Bible, 1846

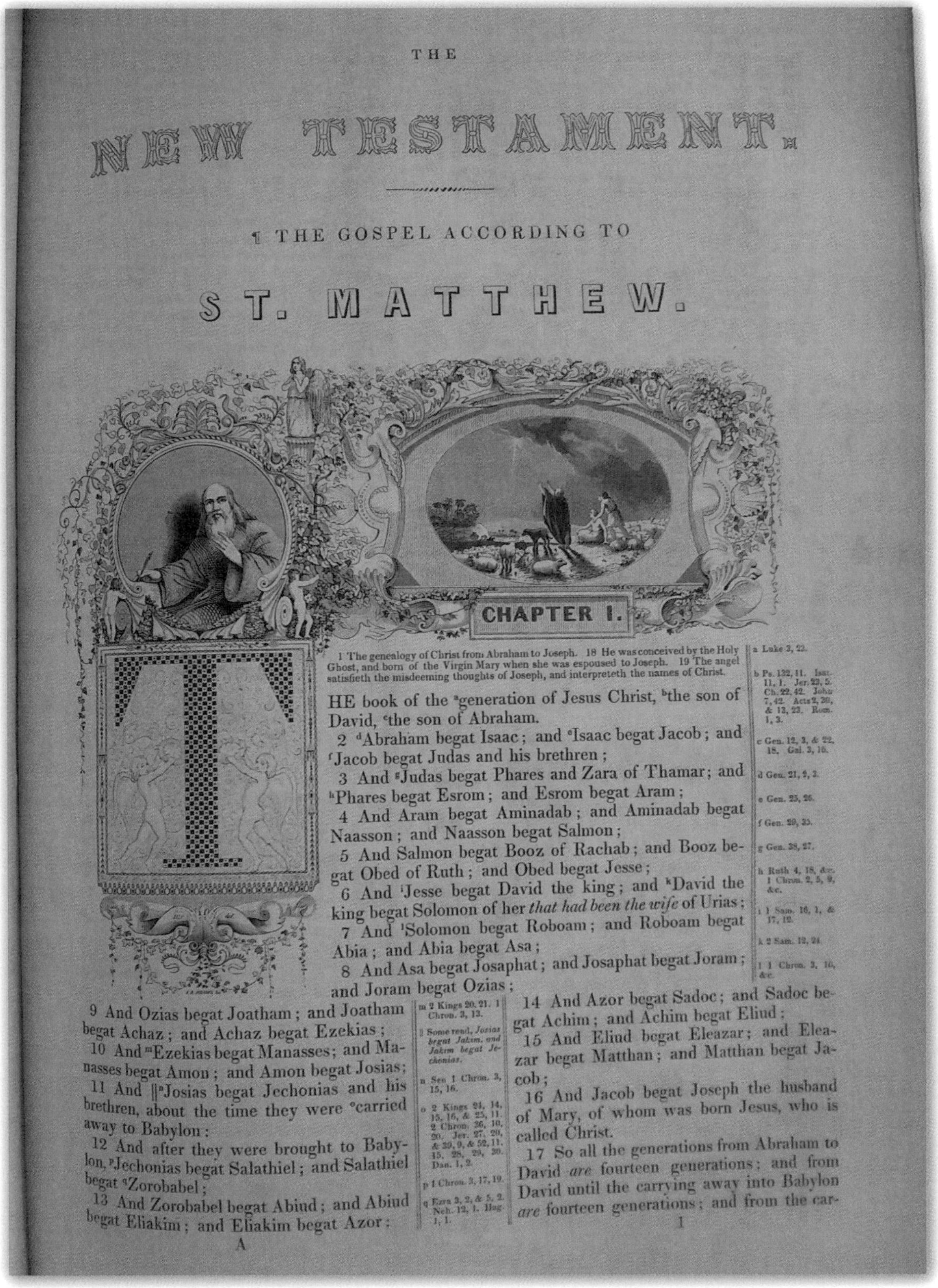

THE

NEW TESTAMENT.

¶ THE GOSPEL ACCORDING TO

ST. MATTHEW.

CHAPTER I.

1 The genealogy of Christ from Abraham to Joseph. 18 He was conceived by the Holy Ghost, and born of the Virgin Mary when she was espoused to Joseph. 19 The angel satisfieth the misdeeming thoughts of Joseph, and interpreteth the names of Christ.

THE book of the [a]generation of Jesus Christ, [b]the son of
David, [c]the son of Abraham.
2 [d]Abraham begat Isaac; and [e]Isaac begat Jacob; and
[f]Jacob begat Judas and his brethren;
3 And [g]Judas begat Phares and Zara of Thamar; and
[h]Phares begat Esrom; and Esrom begat Aram;
4 And Aram begat Aminadab; and Aminadab begat
Naasson; and Naasson begat Salmon;
5 And Salmon begat Booz of Rachab; and Booz begat Obed of Ruth; and Obed begat Jesse;
6 And [i]Jesse begat David the king; and [k]David the
king begat Solomon of her *that had been the wife* of Urias;
7 And [l]Solomon begat Roboam; and Roboam begat
Abia; and Abia begat Asa;
8 And Asa begat Josaphat; and Josaphat begat Joram;
and Joram begat Ozias;
9 And Ozias begat Joatham; and Joatham
begat Achaz; and Achaz begat Ezekias;
10 And [m]Ezekias begat Manasses; and Manasses begat Amon; and Amon begat Josias;
11 And ‖[n]Josias begat Jechonias and his
brethren, about the time they were [o]carried
away to Babylon:
12 And after they were brought to Babylon, [p]Jechonias begat Salathiel; and Salathiel
begat [q]Zorobabel;
13 And Zorobabel begat Abiud; and Abiud
begat Eliakim; and Eliakim begat Azor;
14 And Azor begat Sadoc; and Sadoc begat Achim; and Achim begat Eliud;
15 And Eliud begat Eleazar; and Eleazar begat Matthan; and Matthan begat Jacob;
16 And Jacob begat Joseph the husband
of Mary, of whom was born Jesus, who is
called Christ.
17 So all the generations from Abraham to
David *are* fourteen generations; and from
David until the carrying away into Babylon
are fourteen generations; and from the car-

a Luke 3, 23.
b Ps. 132, 11. Isa. 11, 1. Jer. 23, 5. Ch. 22, 42. John 7, 42. Acts 2, 30, & 13, 23. Rom. 1, 3.
c Gen. 12, 3, & 22, 18. Gal. 3, 16.
d Gen. 21, 2, 3.
e Gen. 25, 26.
f Gen. 29, 35.
g Gen. 38, 27.
h Ruth 4, 18, &c. 1 Chron. 2, 5, 9, &c.
i 1 Sam. 16, 1, & 17, 12.
k 2 Sam. 12, 24.
l 1 Chron. 3, 10, &c.
m 2 Kings 20, 21. 1 Chron. 3, 13.
‖ Some read, *Josias begat Jakim, and Jakim begat Jechonias.*
n See 1 Chron. 3, 15, 16.
o 2 Kings 24, 14, 15, 16, & 25, 11. 2 Chron. 36, 10, 20. Jer. 27, 20, & 39, 9, & 52, 11, 15, 28, 29, 30. Dan. 1, 2.
p 1 Chron. 3, 17, 19.
q Ezra 3, 2, & 5, 2. Neh. 12, 1. Hag. 1, 1.

A

1

1. In their early "ministry of the Word," apostles grouped together, in more or less fixed form, remembrances of what Jesus did and taught. Contemplation in hindsight (John 2:22; 12:16), combined with help from the Holy Spirit on their powers of remembrance (John 14:26), brought clarity and systematic presentation to the collective memory of the apostles. This is reflected, to some degree, in the earliest sermons recorded in Acts (cf. Acts 10:36–40) and in scattered allusions in the epistles (cf. 2 Pet 1:17–18). Notwithstanding slight variations of individual perspective and diversity of personal recollection, the stories and teachings of Christ must have taken on something of a standardized form in the earliest apostolic teaching.

2. Aramaic terms were recast in the Greek language—including established equivalents for words hard to translate. This helps to explain the striking resemblances in points of detail in the various Gospels—including word-for-word correspondence in Greek translation of difficult Aramaic phrases. It also allows for a degree of flexibility with regard to incidental points of differing perspectives, as one would expect with multiple eyewitnesses.

3. Many undertook to "compile an account," or collection, however incomplete, of the sayings and/or deeds of Jesus (Luke 1:1). It is reasonable to assume, in light of Luke's prologue, that various collections of narratives were put to writing at an early period, under the superintendence of the apostles. The Gospels as we now have them were probably not produced, in their present form, until about three decades had elapsed after the resurrection of Christ. One can imagine, however, the intense hunger among the earliest saints for written collections of anecdotes, parables, and events from the life of their Savior. Even in the epistle of 1 Corinthians, Paul alludes to the post-resurrection appearances (1 Cor 15), the institution of the Lord's Supper (1 Cor 11), and to Jesus' personal teaching on divorce (1 Cor 7:10–11). Such scattered allusions, however fragmentary, must have been cherished among early Christians. Whatever incomplete narratives may have existed, none were adequate to the greatness of their subject. Luke sensed this void and the need for a more comprehensive account (Luke 1:1–4).

4. The Gospels as we know them were drawn up. It is not necessary to assume fraudulent copying when the four accounts largely agree, nor is it necessary to assume contradictions are at work when slightly different perspectives of the same episode are expressed. As four independent accounts of essentially the same events, the Gospels overlap at key points and diverge at times, just as one would surmise when viewing four camera angles of an identical photo object. The apostles and other "ministers of the Word" drew from a carefully established body of facts—enhanced by personal reminiscence, the testimony of multiple eyewitnesses, and the infallible guidance of the Spirit—concerning "all that Jesus began to do and teach" (Acts 1:1). They were guardians of a sacred trust, and they faithfully passed on to us an incalculable treasure. The purpose of these efforts, as Luke says, is "that you might know the exact truth about the things you have been taught" (Luke 1:4). John says it this way:

> Many other signs therefore Jesus also performed in the presence of the disciples, which are not written in this book; but these have been written that you may believe that Jesus is the Christ, the Son of God; and that believing you may have life in his name (John 20:30–31).

A scribe at work. Book of Hours, Use of Rome, 1505.

Questions

1. What is the difference between a legend and a historical report?

2. Did the apostles recognize the difference in the preceding question? If so, what measures were taken to safeguard and verify the authenticity of the reports? 2 Pet 1:16

3. How do fairy tales typically begin? Is this the kind of language we read in the Gospel of Luke? Luke 2:1–2; 3:1–2

4. Some critics accuse the Gospel accounts of collusion whenever there is agreement among them, and of discrepancies when there is the slightest point of apparent disagreement. How might this approach be misleading?

5. This lesson has focused on the formation of the Gospels. Yet working backward in time, many of the same principles are at work. The Book of Isaiah is essentially an anthology of the prophet's life work and his prophetic ministry. What possible light does Isaiah 8:16 shed on the "organization" of this material?

Helpful References

Robert H. Stein, *Studying the Synoptic Gospels: Origin and Interpretation*, 2nd ed. Grand Rapids, MI: Baker Academic, 2001. Revised edition of The Synoptic Problem (1987).

Eta Linnemann, *Historical Criticism of the Bible: Methodology or Ideology?* Grand Rapids, MI: Baker Book House, 1990.

Eta Linnemann, *Is There a Synoptic Problem?* Grand Rapids, MI: Baker Book House, 1992.

Craig Blomberg, *The Historical Reliability of the Gospels*. 2nd ed. Downers Grove, IL: IVP Academic, 2007.

Duane Garrett, *Rethinking Genesis*. Grand Rapids, MI: Baker Book House, 1991.

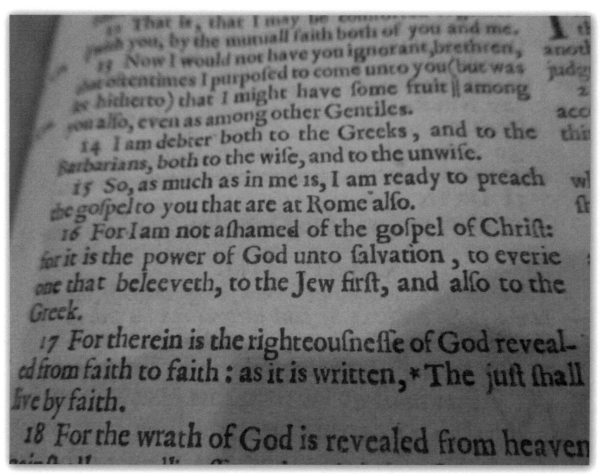

That is, that I may be comforted together with you, by the mutuall faith both of you and me.

13 Now I would not have you ignorant, brethren, that oftentimes I purposed to come unto you (but was let hitherto) that I might have some fruit ‖ among you also, even as among other Gentiles.

14 I am debter both to the Greeks, and to the Barbarians, both to the wise, and to the unwise.

15 So, as much as in me is, I am ready to preach the gospel to you that are at Rome also.

16 For I am not ashamed of the gospel of Christ: for it is the power of God unto salvation, to everie one that beleeveth, to the Jew first, and also to the Greek.

17 For therein is the righteousnesse of God revealed from faith to faith: as it is written, * The just shall live by faith.

18 For the wrath of God is revealed from heaven

Romans 1:16–17 in the King's English, 1629

LESSON 3
Publishing the Message

Oral Publication

Ancient poets and philosophers—including notables such as Homer and Socrates—published their works by proclaiming them orally. Pindar wrote lyric poems to be recited for athletic champions when they returned from the games. Jesus also published the good news by oral proclamation and never personally wrote out his sermons, as far as we know. Just as Plato preserved the teachings of his mentor, Socrates, Jesus' disciples were commissioned to safeguard the teachings of Jesus.

Even when such messages were later recorded for posterity, the compositions were structured more for the ears than the eyes. Repetition of key terms would help listeners follow the line of thought. For example, in the Sermon on the Mount, Jesus repeats the formula, "You have heard that it was said … But I say to you …" (Matt 5:21–48). These and other transition markers helped hearers follow the main points.

The role of a king's "herald" was to go from town to town throughout the realm announcing royal proclamations. Thus, in biblical times, publication was as much "oral" as it was "written," even when a message was put to writing. In Galatians 6:6, both the one "who is taught" and the "one who teaches" translate a form of the Greek word *katēcheō*, from which the later Roman Catholic tradition of "catechism" is derived. In the New Testament period, this term was used of "oral proclamation … a teacher rehearsing Jesus' words and deeds, with the congregation orally repeating what was taught and committing it to memory. (This was the way nearly all teaching occurred in Hellenistic times)" (Philip Comfort, *Encountering the Manuscripts*, p. 3).

In the case of the Gospels, we should understand that the basic information was made available orally for many years before the written text came to market (see Lesson 2). When it comes to the shift between *oral proclamation* and *the Gospels as we now*

have them (in writing), we might think in terms of releasing a new edition of a book in a repackaged format. This is why Luke says, "Many have undertaken to compile a narrative" of these things prior to the existence of "many" Gospel accounts in their present form (Luke 1:1).

Transcription

In order to make available widespread, long-term access to the Word of God, the message had to be chronicled in written form. Concerning the interplay between "oral" and "written" communication, Paul writes,

> So then, brothers, stand firm and hold to the traditions that you were taught by us, either by our spoken word or by our letter (2 Thess 2:15).

In light of his imminent death by execution, after which face-to-face oral instruction would no longer be possible, Peter hastened to put material into writing, "so that after my departure you may be able at any time to recall these things" (2 Pet 1:14–15). In the same epistle, he alludes to Paul and "all his letters" along with "the other Scriptures" (3:15–16). It is possible that a bound collection of Paul's epistles was already circulating, but at minimum, they were already somewhat widespread and recognized as Scripture. This is remarkable, first, because all copying and distribution involved a slow, painstaking process; and second, because the lag time between publication of Paul's letters and the writing of 2 Peter would have been short.

When a New Testament Gospel or epistle was published, there were several key steps.

First, the author would write a book. Oftentimes books (especially letters) were dictated to an *amanuensis* (or scribe), who would record the speaker's words, perhaps in shorthand, and then produce a transcript, which the author could review, edit, correct, and sign in his own handwriting. Paul dictated Romans to Tertius (Rom 16:22) and Peter dictated 1 Peter to Silvanus (or Silas) (1 Pet 5:12). The Gospel of Mark probably preserves the oral teaching of Peter, written by Mark, as early Christian

opposite page
Table of the four Gospels, book of Kells (c. A.D. 800)

history attests. In some cases, the scribe may have also translated or slightly polished dictated thoughts before the writer signed off on the original text. This may account for stylistic differences between 1 and 2 Peter, or differences between the Johannine writings and the Book of Revelation. Paul evidently dictated several epistles and signed the closing salutation with his own hand (Gal 6:11; 2 Thess 3:17). This special calligraphy would have been a safeguard of authenticity to the original recipients.

In some cases, there was an intermediate editing process. For some New Testament books, there may have been little difference between the authorized autograph and the published text. Galatians was written in the heat of the moment, with little or no editing. On the other hand, the four Gospels, Romans, Hebrews, and 1 Peter were written for wide original audiences and may have undergone editorial revision. In such cases, the original autograph would be tantamount to a "first draft." The Book of Revelation appears to have been recorded by John as he saw the visions (see 10:4), and then he published it (quickly?) in a style that seems less grammatically polished than the Gospel or epistles that bear his name. Some have suggested that John 21 may have been added in a second edition of the Fourth Gospel, after a more natural ending of 20:30–31. John 21:24 adds, "And we know that his testimony is true." Is this the voice of authorized editors, trusted disciples, or perhaps, as some believe, the Ephesian elders?

After editing was complete, a published archetype was produced. Philip Comfort writes,

> The handwriting of archetypal texts is a different story than the autographs because published archetypal texts would normally have a polished look to them (*Encountering*, p. 10).

This was a "master copy" from which additional copies would be made for distribution. In some cases, there was likely a wealthy patron who sponsored or funded the enterprise at the outset. Theophilus may have filled this role for Luke and Acts, since both of these books are dedicated to him (Luke 1:3; Acts 1:1).

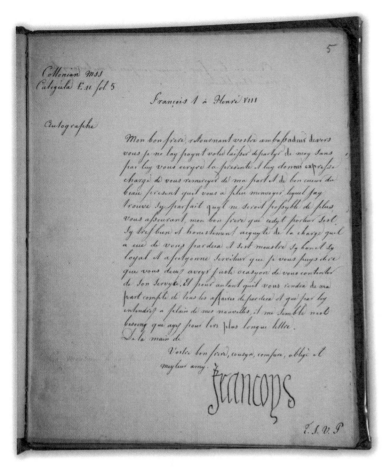

Many New Testament documents were similarly transcribed, then signed by the author at the end. This is a letter from the King of France to Henry VIII of England.

Delivery

There was no official postal system for the masses in the Roman Empire. Letter writers put their communiques into the hands of trusted envoys. This served two purposes. First, this was a form of "certified mail" delivery to a destination, so that the intended recipients would indeed receive their mail. Second, the one transporting the document had the additional role of verifying the circumstances of its origin and of filling in any additional details. The New Testament is full of intriguing clues describing this process (Rom 16:1–2; 1 Cor 4:17; Col 4:7–18; etc.). One of the best-known examples is found near the end of Ephesians.

So that you also may know how I am and what I am doing, Tychicus the beloved brother and faithful minister in the Lord will tell you everything. I have sent him for this very purpose, that you may know how we are, and that he may encourage your hearts (Eph 6:21–22).

Questions

1. We think of a published work as something written down, but the ancients were not always literate, and oral communication was highly valued. Yet even today, digital recordings are (somewhat) copyright protected as "intellectual" or "artistic" property. How can "oral publication" impact our understanding of the process?

2. Is there any difference in the authority of the spoken word versus the written word? 2 Thess 2:15

3. List the three potential stages of publishing a New Testament document.
   a.

b.

c.

4. What two important roles did a letter-bearer have in New Testament times?

5. It is also possible that the one transporting a document could be commissioned to read it to the intended recipients upon his arrival. In this way, he could "represent" the author and stand in his place as the document was read. Some believe that the "angels of the seven churches" in Revelation were actually *human messengers* who fulfilled this role. In any case, imagine being in a first-century congregation and hearing the words, "Blessed is the one who reads aloud the words of this prophecy, and blessed are those who hear, and who keep what is written in it, for the time is near" (Rev 1:3).

Helpful References

Philip W. Comfort, *Encountering the Manuscripts: An Introduction to New Testament Paleography and Textual Criticism*. Nashville, TN: Broadman & Holman, 2005.

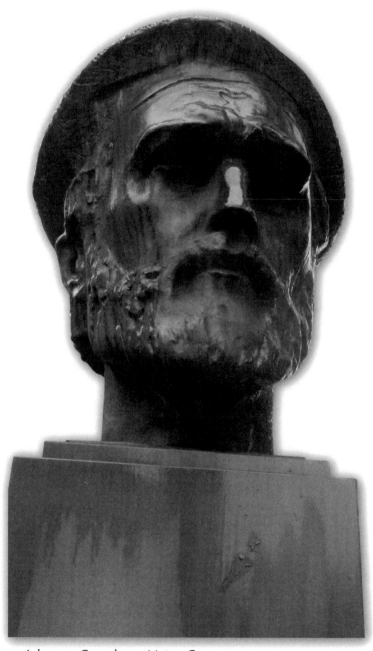

Johannes Gutenberg, Mainz, Germany

LESSON 4
Preserving the Message

Those who transported the New Testament documents delivered them into the hands of trusted recipients. The original recipients, in turn, had a sacred responsibility to safeguard the message, to certify the contents, and to begin the circulation process.

The prayer book of a young Englishwoman, 18th century, with sharkskin cover and clasps.

Deposit

None of the original autograph documents of New Testament books has survived to the present day, as far as we know. Had any of them lasted through the ages, they would probably be treated as relics and objects of worship. However, the essential content of each document has been preserved. In the case of the epistles, a "master copy" in many cases would have been produced by a scribe, with the writer's personal signature and closing greetings at the end (see discussion on pages 20–21).

Before the discovery of the Dead Sea Scrolls in 1947, the only manuscript of the Old Testament older than the time of Christ was the Nash papyrus, 1st or 2nd century B.C.

After writing his last preserved letter, Paul instructs his younger protégé, Timothy, "By the Holy Spirit who dwells within us, guard the good deposit entrusted to you" (2 Tim 1:14). This might mean that Timothy is to hold fast to the pure teaching without deviation. However, it may indicate more than that, as some have suggested—that Timothy was the designated appointee or "trustee" of Paul's life work; i.e. he had the task of preserving, organizing, and combining Paul's epistles into a single collection, and in light of his impending departure (4:6–8), Paul was giving Timothy a final charge to be faithful to the task.

At the very least, those privileged to receive the autographed original documents were entrusted with a vitally important mission. The first copies of the writings that would later form a complete New Testament must be accepted, read, safely stored, and then copied for a wider audience. The same process occurred with the Old Testament documents (Deut 31:24–26; Josh 24:26–27; 1 Sam 10:25).

Certification

From Old Testament times, prophets were authenticated by the power of God that accompanied their message. Moses used his rod to display the "finger of God" (Ex 8:19). Elisha performed miracles (2 Kings 5:8). Jeremiah uttered both short-term and long-term predictive prophecies, which were fulfilled in stunning detail (cf. Jer 28). This is one reason we read the Book of Jeremiah and not a book produced by his rival, Hananiah (see Jer 28:16–17)! Jesus performed indisputable "signs" (John 20:30–31). The apostles' message was "confirmed" by miracles (Heb 2:3–4). As already noted in Lesson 1, false prophets were unable to compete (Deut 18:22).

As for the written documents of the New Testament, there were two ways of certifying the contents as apostolic or as a legitimate part of God's revelation. One was a "spiritual" factor, and the other was part of the "material" evidence.

Spiritually, there was the gift of "discerning of spirits" (1 Cor 12:10). Just as "various kinds of tongues" are paired with "the interpretation of tongues," the gift of "prophecy" is conjoined with "the ability to distinguish between the spirits." In this way, there would be spiritual checks and balances on any presumed revelation from God (1 John 4:1). Paul says,

> If anyone thinks that he is a prophet, or spiritual, he should acknowledge that the things I am writing to you are a command of the Lord. If anyone does not recognize this, he is not recognized (1 Cor 14:37–38).

This same authenticating process is under consideration in 1 Thess 5:19–21.

> Do not quench the Spirit. Do not despise prophecies, but test everything: hold fast to what is good. Abstain from every form of evil.

Those with the gift of "discerning of spirits" were on hand to verify a true word of God and differentiate it from anything counterfeit.

Materially, as already noted, Paul dictated several epistles and signed the closing salutation with his own hand (Gal 6:11; 2 Thess 3:17). This special calligraphy would have been an additional safeguard of authenticity to the original recipients. Ancient Christians were well aware of the difference between a forgery and a genuine article. Paul urges the Thessalonians

> not to be quickly shaken in mind or alarmed, either by a spirit or a spoken word, or a letter seeming to be from us, to the effect that the day of the Lord has come. Let no one deceive you in any way… (2 Thess 2:2–3).

This is the background behind his closing signature—

> I, Paul, write this greeting with my own hand. This is the sign of genuineness in every letter of mine; it is the way I write (2 Thess 3:17).

Finally, as mentioned in the previous lesson, those entrusted with hand-delivering a document or letter were also entrusted with filling in details about its production, as well as conveying additional information concerning the author (Eph 6:21–22). In tandem with factors mentioned above, this would remove any

The John Rylands fragment of the Gospel of John, early second century

doubt about the circumstances of a document's origin. In a few cases, there would be a follow-up visit from the writer himself, providing further confirmation—

> I had much to write to you, but I would rather not write with pen and ink. I hope to see you soon, and we will talk face to face (3 John 13–14).

Reproduction and Circulation

Most of the New Testament documents were faithfully copied and widely circulated almost immediately. Embedded in some of the books themselves are solemn instructions to do this very thing.

- ▶ I put you under oath before the Lord to have this letter read to all the brothers (1 Thess 5:27).

- ▶ And when this letter has been read among you, have it also read in the church of the Laodiceans; and see that you also read the letter from Laodicea (Col 4:16).

- ▶ I warn everyone who hears the words of the prophecy of this book: if anyone adds to them, God will add to him the plagues described in this book, and if anyone takes away from the words of the book of this prophecy, God will take away his share in the tree of life and in the holy city, which are described in this book (Rev 22:18–19).

Questions

1. Someone says, "The writers of the New Testament had no idea that the documents they produced would be circulated so widely." How would you refute this assertion?

2. What does Matt 24:15 imply about how recipients would receive Jesus' warning of a future destruction of Jerusalem?

3. What does Rev 1:3 imply about what occurred when a congregation received such a document as this?

4. What responsibilities did the original recipients have when they received an autographed original of a New Testament book?

5. How did the original audience know that a letter coming from Paul was the real thing, and not a forgery?

6. What does Rev 22:18–19 imply about the copying process?

7. The apostle Peter wrote, "But the word of the Lord remains (abides) forever" (1 Pet 1:25). Jesus also promised, "Heaven and earth will pass away, but my words will not pass away" (Matt 24:25). What do these two passages suggest about God's role in the preservation of Scripture?

The prophecie

The booke of the prophete Esai.

The first Chapter.

2 The prophete accuseth the sinnes of the people : namely of ingratefulnesse, stubburnesse, 11 faythlesse seruice of God, 24 and sheweth Gods terrible iudgement agaynst them, vnlesse they repent.

THE (a) vision of Esai the sonne of Amos, which he sawe vpon Juda and Hierusalem, in the dayes of Uzia & Joathan, Ahaz and Jehezekiah, kinges of Juda. Heare O hea-

sed, and euery hart heauie:

6 From the sole of the foote, vnto the head there is nothing sounde in it : [but] woundes, blaynes, and putrifieyng sore : they haue not benne salued, neyther wrapped vp, neyther molified with the oyntment.

7 Your land is wasted, your cities are burnt vp, strangers deuour your lande before your face, and it is made desolate, as it were the destruction of enimies [in the tyme of warre.

8 And the daughter of Sion shalbe left as

Opening page of Isaiah, Bishops' Bible, 1572

32

LESSON 5
The Concept of a Book

The word *Bible* comes from *biblia*, "books" in Latin and Greek. It was God's intention from the beginning to bequeath a "Book of books" to the world. As human civilization developed, so did the process of writing and components of book manufacture, making the very idea of a God-given Book possible.

Language and Writing

The written recording of human language first took shape in the form of pictures. Eventually these pictorial representations grew more complex and standardized, as in Sumerian cuneiform script or Egyptian hieroglyphics. Finally, the pictures were reduced to alphabetic symbols, in which more complex combinations of written communication could occur. One scholar, Douglas Petrovich, has recently argued that the earliest known alphabet was, in fact, an early version of the Hebrew language.

Epic of Gilgamesh in cuneiform

Proto-Sinaitic Script, an early alphabet form

Very early writing, Kish Tablet from Sumer, 3500 B.C.

Lachish ostracon replica, Hebrew script on a potsherd

The Cyrus Cylinder, made of baked clay, measures nearly 9 inches long and 4 inches wide at its maximum diameter

Book Formats in the Ancient World

Book technology is changing fast. Although the physical book is never going to be completely replaced, electronic books have become commonplace. Many eBooks are interactive, with audio and video links built into them.

In ancient times, written communication took shape as inscriptions on monuments, *ostraca* (broken pots), and various other materials seen as museum artifacts today. A person's personal identification was impressed from pictographs of a seal onto clay. Depending on the period and region, people wrote on papyrus, clay, wood, parchment (leather), or wax tablets.

During much of biblical history, we should think of a "scroll" when we read the term "book" (cf. Rev 5). Eventually, the Roman world gave birth to the codex, which was a precursor to the modern book. Several folded sheets of parchment or vellum (high-quality calf skin) would be folded together and bound on one end, with a thicker cover encasing the contents. Early Christians preferred the codex to the scroll. One reason was the compact user-friendliness of it. The Gospel of Luke would take up about 31 feet of scroll—cumbersome and impractical—but all four Gospels could fit into a codex.

Sinaiticus and Alexandrinus

On the other hand, there was a high cost involved. Producing a "manuscript" (literally something that is "hand-written") is labor intensive. Moreover, the average calfskin produced only three-and-a-half medium-sized sheets of writing material, so a lot of animals had to be slaughtered to produce a full-size book.

The "Canon" of Holy Scripture

How do we know the 66 books of the Bible belong in the sacred text as part of "God's Book" and that they are the *only* writings that should be included? What about the *Apocrypha* or the *Gnostic Gospels*? You may have seen an ad peddling the "Secret Teachings of Jesus" or the "Lost Books of the Bible." The answer lies in the *canon*, a word derived from Greek which means "rod" or "rule." As applied to the books of the Bible, it means the rule or standard applied to the writings, which are recognized as Holy Scripture.

Many discussions in the early centuries of the church were devoted to this topic, especially in an environment in which heretics accepted certain uninspired books or rejected certain genuine ones. For example, Marcion (c. A.D. 110–160) accepted only the epistles of Paul. The Gnostics, on the other hand, had their own writings such as the so-called *Gospel of Thomas*, the *Gospel of Mary Magdalene*, and the *Gospel of Judas*.

1. Looking Backward—Criteria for Inclusion. It is important to realize that the early church did not *determine* which books were inspired and which were not. The main issue was *recognizing* what God had already determined when he revealed his truth through chosen men. Formal sanction in later centuries simply acknowledged writings that were long since widely accepted in the churches. Athanasius in A.D. 367, Jerome's Latin Vulgate (c. A.D. 385), and the councils at Hippo (A.D. 393) and Carthage (A.D. 397) all recognized the same 27 books that are found in our present New Testament.

The discussions of later years focused on five criteria:

- ▸ **Apostolic Test.** Was it written by or in connection with an apostle? For example, Mark was closely associated with Peter, and Luke with Paul.
- ▸ **Doctrinal Test.** Did it conform to apostolic teaching, or did it promote a heretical doctrine? (Gal 1:8–9)
- ▸ **Age Test.** Was it written in the New Testament period? The Shepherd of Hermas was a popular book among Christians in the second and third centuries, but it was written in the middle

of the second century, in the post-apostolic age, and therefore excluded. The assumption was that the faith was "once for all delivered to the saints" in the first century (Jude 3), and, once delivered, fully complete (2 Tim 3:16–17; 2 Pet 1:3).

- ▸ **"Catholic" (Universal) Test.** Was it widely acknowledged by the church at large, or was it only a "local" favorite? (In this connection, "catholic" = "universal.")

- ▸ **Inspiration Test.** The bottom line, even if an apostle did not write it: Was it given under the direction of the Holy Spirit as part of "God-breathed" Scripture (2 Tim 3:16–17)?

It should be mentioned that Christians in the late first and second centuries were already on record with discussions of the background of various books. Clement, Ignatius, Papias, Irenaeus, and other "church fathers" weighed in on the subject. *The Muratorian fragment* (c. A.D. 170) is perhaps the oldest known list of New Testament books (and the text is available online). It corresponds fairly closely to our present list, with a few minor variations, and represents a time when the canon was not quite universally fixed. The process of collecting a few of the books was evidently still going on in some places, and questions were raised about a few books. Even still, it bears a striking resemblance to a modern listing of New Testament books.

2. Looking Forward—Putting the Books into One Collection. Most discussions of the canon view the issue in hindsight, looking back at the apostolic age from the time of later councils. Perhaps instead we should look from the biblical period forward, since there are clues in the Bible itself regarding how God's Word should be put together (Isa 8:16; Jer 36:32; et al.). Again, there are five tests that give "advance notice" about inspired writings.

- ▸ **Was it written by a prophet of God?** I.e., is it genuinely inspired? (Deut 18:18; 2 Pet 1:20–21). For N.T. documents, do they bear apostolic authority? (Heb 1:1–2)

- ▸ **Was he confirmed by an act of God?** Moses used his rod to display the "finger of God" (Ex 8:19). Elisha performed miracles (2 Kings 5:8). Jeremiah uttered both short-term and long-term predictive prophecies, which were fulfilled in stunning detail (cf. Jer 28). Jesus performed indisputable "signs" (John 20:30–31).

The apostles' message was "confirmed" by miracles (Heb 2:3–4). False prophets were unable to compete (Deut 18:22). Remember also that for N.T. period prophecies, there was also the spiritual gift of "discerning of spirits" (1 Cor 12:10; 1 Thess 5:19–21).

▸ **Does his message harmonize with prior revelations of God?** A new revelation builds on and is an extension of prior revelations. It may contain some new information, but it cannot contradict legitimate revelations in the past (Gal 1:8). Even if a false prophet seemed to meet criterion #2, he would fail this one and must be rejected (Deut 13:1–5).

▸ **Does it have the power of God?** Anyone familiar with the Apocryphal Gospels is able to sense the overwhelming difference between them and the four canonical Gospels (John 7:17). The counterfeit is vastly inferior to the real thing. For example, the Gospel of Thomas says, "Simon Peter said to them, 'Make Mary leave us, for females don't deserve life.' Jesus said, 'Look, I will guide her to make her male, so that she too may become a living spirit resembling you males. For every female who makes herself male will enter the kingdom of Heaven.'" (114) The Infancy Gospel of Thomas mentions a childhood incident in which Jesus strikes a Pharisee dead for emptying his pool of water (3). There is a sense of dignity, reserve, trustworthiness and power in the genuine Word that is missing from the pretenders (Heb 4:12).

▸ **Was it accepted by the people of God?** Throughout the history of divine revelation, measures have been taken by God to ensure that the original recipients of his message recognize it as such and circulate it accordingly (as outlined in Lesson 4).

▷ It should be recognized as "the Word of God" (1 Thess 2:13).

▷ Instructions are given for perpetuation "markers" and repository (Deut 31:24–26; Josh 24:26–27; 1 Sam 10:25).

▷ Biblical writers formally recognize other inspired writers (Dan 9:2; 2 Pet 3:16; 1 Tim 5:8).

▷ The people of God were to publish and circulate legitimate written revelations (Col 4:16; 1 Thess 5:27; 2 Thess 2:2; 3:17; Eph 6:21–22).

The bottom line in all of this is that there are no "lost books" of the Bible. Certain works were rejected as apocryphal ("hidden away") or pseudepigraphal ("falsely attributed" to someone

Scribe writing

noteworthy). As the councils of Hippo and Carthage both con-
cluded, "And further it was resolved that nothing should be read
in church under the name of the divine scriptures except the canonical writings. The canonical writings, then, are these..." A list
of our present New Testament books follows.

Questions

1. What is the "canon" of Scripture?

2. The Bible contains two "testaments" (or "covenants") with 39 "books" in the Old Testament and 27 in the New Testament. How do the following passages clarify our understanding of God's Book?

   a. Luke 24:44–45

   b. John 1:17

   c. Hebrews 8:6–13

   d. Revelation 22:18–19

3. What factors determined whether a document belonged as a book in the Bible?

Helpful References

Douglas Petrovich, *The World's Oldest Alphabet: Hebrew As The Language of the Proto-Consonantal Script.* Jerusalem: Carta, 2016.

Keith Houston, *The Book: A Cover-To-Cover Exploration of the Most Powerful Object of Our Time.* New York: Norton & Company, 2016.

Any good Bible dictionary will have an article on the Canon and related topics (such as "Apocrypha").

F. F. Bruce. *The Canon of Scripture.* Downers Grove, IL: Inter-Varsity Press, 1988.

Der Prophet Zephania.

1.

Is ist das wort des HE-
RRN/ welchs geschach zu Zephania
dem son Chusi/ des sons Gedalia/ des
sons Amaria/ des sons Hiskia/ zur zeit
Josia des sons Amon des Königes
Juda.

Ich wil alles aus dem lande weg
nemen/ spricht der HERR/ Ich wil
beide menschen vnd vihe/ beide vogel
des himels vnd fische im meer weg ne
men/ sampt den Götzen vnd den Gott
losen/ Ja/ ich wil die menschen ausreu
ten aus dem lande/ spricht der HERR/ Ich wil meine hand ausstre
cken vber Juda vnd vber alle die zu Jerusalem wonen/ Also wil ich das
vbrige vom Baal ausreuten/ dazu den namen der a Münche vnd Pfaf-
fen aus diesem ort/ vnd die/ so auff den dechern des himels heer anbe-
ten/ Die es anbeten/ vnd schweren doch bey dem HERRN/ vnd zu
gleich bey Malchom/ vnd die vom HERRN abfallen/ vnd die nach
dem HERRN nichts fragen/ vnd jn nicht achten.

Seid stille fur dem HErrn HERRN/ Denn des HERRN tag ist
nahe/ Denn der HERR hat ein schlachtopffer zubereit/ vnd seine b geste dazu geladen/ Vnd am tage des Schlachtopffers des HERRN/
wil ich heimsuchen/ die Fürsten vnd des Königes kinder/ vnd alle die
ein frembd kirchen schmuck tragen/ Auch wil ich zur selbigen zeit/ die
heimsuchen/ so vber die schwelle springen/ die jrer Herrn haus füllen
mit rauben vnd triegen.

Zur selbi-

a
(Münche)
Camarim/ die bes-
ser sein wolten/
denn schlechte pfaf-
fen oder priester/
Vnd Malchom
war ein Abgott/
der kinder Am-
mon.

b
(Geste)
Die Babylonier
so Jerusalem sol-
len fressen / dar-
umb das sie frem-
de weise/ Gott zu
dienen / hielten /
ausser Mose etc.

The Prophet Zephaniah, Luther Bible

LESSON 6
Biblical Authority and Scribal Transmission

How do we know the earliest scribes faithfully reproduced the text in the earliest copies? For starters, there was a long tradition, established from ancient times while the Bible was still being revealed, of *total respect* for the written Word of God. There were to be *no additions or deletions* (Rev 22:18–19; Deut 4:2: 12:32). In this lesson we look at some of this evidence.

Internal Verification

Apart from the external evidence from church history, biblical writers themselves recognize the divine authority in one another's writings. Thus, Daniel recognizes Jeremiah (Dan 9:2), Jeremiah recognizes Micah (Jer 26:18), and the New Testament recognizes "Moses and the prophets" (Luke 16:29; Matt 17:3–5). Peter acknowledges the writings of Paul and equates them with "the other Scriptures" (2 Pet 3:16). In 1 Timothy 5:8, Paul cites both Deut 25:4 and a saying of Jesus (cf. Matt 10:10), introducing both quotations with the words, "For the Scripture says…"

Jesus and the apostles recognize the authority of the Old Testament. For Jesus, the Old Testament was "scripture," "the word of God" (Mark 7:13), and "the law" of God (Luke 10:26). When citing a passage from the Psalms, he inserts the words, "and Scripture cannot be broken" (John 10:35). In the Sermon on the Mount, he affirms his respect for previous revelations of God: "Do not think that I have come to abolish the Law or the Prophets; I have not come to abolish them but to fulfill them. For truly, I say to you, until heaven and earth pass away, not an iota, not a dot, will pass from the Law until all is accomplished" (Matt 5:17–18). Oftentimes he introduces an Old Testament saying with the words, "It is written…" (Matt 4:4, 6–7).

The first lines from Romans 8, Codex Sinaiticus

Evidence from the Early Church

Christians from the early centuries of church history, even outside the New Testament, generally display a high regard for biblical authority. This is consistent with the warning in Revelation 22:18–19 not to "add to" or "take away" from the holy contents. Instilling this kind of respect for the Word of God would have precluded tampering in the scribal transmission of the documents.

> ▸ As all gold, whatsoever it be, that is without the temple, is not holy; even so every notion which is without the divine Scripture, however admirable it may appear to some, is not holy, because it is foreign to Scripture. (Origen, *Hom.* 25 in Matt.)

> ▸ Whence comes this tradition? Does it descend from the Lord's authority, or from the commands and epistles of the apostles? For those things are to be done which are there written… If it be commanded in the gospels or the epistles and Acts of the Apostles, then let this holy tradition be observed. (Cyprian, *Ep. 74 ad Pompeium*)

> ▸ The Catholic Christians will neither speak nor ensure to hear anything in religion that is a stranger to Scripture; it being an evil heart of immodesty to speak those things which are not written. (Athanasius, *Exhort. Ad Monachas*)

> ▸ How can we use those things which we do not find in the Holy Scriptures? (Ambrose, *Ambr. Offic.*, 1:23)

> ▸ We ought not to seek those things that are passed in silence, but rest in the things which are written. (Theodoret, *Questions on Genesis* 45)

The Bible as a Book of Covenants

The most striking feature of the Bible's contents is the division between the Old Covenant, or Testament, and the New Covenant. Covenants contain specific terms and stipulations, so that once parties strike a deal and formalize the agreement, the conditions are not so easily altered after-the-fact. If this is true in human contracts, it is even more relevant when the counterparty is God. The apostle Paul makes the same point when discussing the relationship between the Abrahamic covenant and the Law of Moses:

> To give a human example, brothers: even with a man-made covenant, no one annuls it or adds to it once it has been ratified…

A finely preserved Bishops' Bible, 1572

This is what I mean: the law, which came 430 years afterward, does not annul a covenant previously ratified by God, so as to make the promise void (Gal 3:15, 17).

We should not pass over these words lightly: "No one annuls it or adds to it once it has been ratified." Like the laws of the Medes and Persians alluded to in the Old Testament, "it cannot be revoked." Moreover, when we are dealing with God, "there is no variation or shadow due to change" (James 1:17). We should contemplate long and hard "the unchanging character of his purpose" (Heb 6:17).

In fact, the previously cited verse is found within a paragraph that underscores God's covenant promises and his oath to Abraham (Heb 6:13–20).

The New Covenant is replete with attitudes as well as actions expected of God's people. These include details for personal life, a specific plan of salvation, and a blueprint for the mission and public worship of the church. All of these components are part of our "contract" with God. From ancient times, God's people have known that if they take the promised blessings seriously, they should give equal attention to the terms and conditions. Consequently, early Christian scribes understood the authoritative nature of the message they were copying—*no additions, no deletions, no tampering!*

Evidence Regarding the Transmission of the Old Testament

In modern times, we organize the Old Testament into five categories: five books of Law (the "Pentateuch"), 12 books of History, five books of Wisdom and Poetry, five Major Prophets, and 12 Minor Prophets. From ancient times, however, Jews organized the same books into three sections, as follows:

- ▶ **Law** (*torah*)
  - ▷ Genesis, Exodus, Leviticus, Numbers, Deuteronomy
- ▶ **Prophets** (*nevi'im*)
  - ▷ Former Prophets (Joshua, Judges, Samuel, Kings)
  - ▷ Later Prophets (Isaiah, Jeremiah, Ezekiel, 12 minor prophets)
- ▶ **Writings** (*ketuvim*)
  - ▷ Psalms, Job, Proverbs, Ruth, Song of Solomon, Ecclesiastes, Lamentations, Esther, Daniel, Ezra, Nehemiah, Chronicles

Notice the Hebrew names of the three sections are *torah, nevi'im,* and *ketuvim.* The first letters of each section form the acronym **Tanakh**, with vowels to help with pronunciation.

- ▶ **T**orah—Law
- ▶ **N**evi'im—Prophets
- ▶ **K**etuvim—Writings

One might say that in the three sections, the Lord is doing three things:

- ▶ **Law**—God teaches us
- ▶ **Prophets**—God shows us through history and preaching
- ▶ **Writings**—God stirs us with examples of how faith works in the real world

Interestingly enough, the first-century Jewish historian, Josephus, alludes to the three sections. Jesus does as well, in Luke 24:44— "Then he said to them, 'These are my words that I spoke to you while I was still with you, that everything written about me in the Law of Moses and the Prophets and the Psalms must be fulfilled.'" (He calls the third part, "the Psalms," after the name of the first and most prominent book in the series).

Jewish scribes had a process for copying the text that reflected this total respect for authority. Every copy of every manuscript was painstakingly written out by hand. To prevent scribal errors in synagogue copies, the following rules were adopted:

- ▶ Each scribe would make sure his reed pen functioned well by dipping it in ink, writing "Amalek," and then crossing it out (cf. Deut 25:19).

- ▶ Parchments had to be made of clean animals (kosher), and feather quills had to be crafted from clean birds. The ink must be black and made to specification.

- ▶ No word or even letter could be written from memory. A scribe must have another scroll before him and pronounce every word out loud before copying it.

- ▶ Before writing the name of God, a scribe must wipe his pen and say, "I am writing the name of God for the holiness of his name."

- ▶ Every letter had to have some space around it. If one letter touched another, or if any defect occurred via hole, tear, or smudge, the scroll was invalidated.

- ▶ Each column must have no fewer than 48 nor more than 60 lines, and it must be identical to the manuscript from which it was copied.

- ▶ Within 30 days of completion, an editor would review the manuscript, counting every letter and word. He would also check to make sure the middle word on each page matched the one from the manuscript being copied.

▸ Up to three mistakes on any page could be corrected within 30 days. If more mistakes were found or remained uncorrected within 30 days, the entire manuscript was burned. If a single letter was added or left out, the manuscript had to be fixed or buried.

Unfortunately, most good Hebrew manuscripts of the Old Testament date from the Middle Ages. However, these can be cross-checked with the following sources:

▸ Copies of the Septuagint, or Greek translation of the Hebrew Scriptures (completed in the third century B.C.);

▸ Copies of the Samaritan Pentateuch;

▸ Portions of the Old Testament found among the Dead Sea Scrolls;

▸ Copies of the Old Testament by Christian scribes in various languages (Greek, Latin, etc.).

Among the Dead Sea Scrolls, discovered in 1947, is a complete scroll of Isaiah. It predates Jesus Christ and dates from perhaps the second century B.C. Except for a few scribal errors, its text is identical to the text of Isaiah in the oldest previously known Hebrew manuscript from A.D. 850—*a thousand years later!*

The Dead Sea Scrolls were arguably the most spectacular archaeological discovery of the 20th century

Questions

1. We sometimes discuss how biblical authority affects our own beliefs and practices. What impact did the authoritative nature of the Bible have on the earliest scribes who hand-copied it?

2. How does the "covenant" structure of the Bible factor in the way we read it or the respect we should have for it?

3. The principles in this lesson are anticipated in Deuteronomy with regard to future kings of Israel—"And when he sits on the throne of his kingdom, *he shall write for himself in a book a copy of this law, approved by the Levitical priests.* And it shall be with him, and he shall read in it all the days of his life, that he may learn to fear the Lord his God by keeping all the words of this law and these statutes, and doing them, that his heart may not be lifted up above his brothers, and that he may not turn aside from the commandment, either to the right hand or to the left, so that he may continue long in his kingdom, he and his children, in Israel" (Deut 17:18–20, emphasis added). Why do you suppose the king's copy had to be approved by the Levitical priests? (cf. Deut 33:10; Ezra 7:10; 2 Chron 15:3; 17:7–9)

4. What, in your opinion, is the most thought-provoking point made in this lesson?

Helpful References

Larry Stone, *The Story of the Bible: The Fascinating History Of Its Writing, Translation & Effect On Civilization*. Nashville, TN: Thomas Nelson, 2010.

Edward D. Andrews. *Misrepresenting Jesus: Debunking Bart D. Ehrman's "Misquoting Jesus."* 3rd ed. Cambridge, OH: Christian Publishing House, 2017.

Mike Wilson, *Inside Out: The New Covenant Written on the Heart*. Posey-Wilson Publishing Group, 2015.

LESSON 7

The Manuscripts— Can We Trust Them?

Bart Ehrman of the University of North Carolina (Chapel Hill) has made a career out of bashing the integrity and divine origin of the Bible. Although he is a respected scholar and gifted writer, he obviously has an axe to grind against the evangelical faith he once accepted as a youth. Here are a few representative quotations from his *Misquoting Jesus: The Story Behind Who Changed the Bible and Why* (2005):

- ► We have only error ridden copies, and the vast majority of these are centuries removed from the originals and different from them, evidently, in thousands of ways. (p. 7)

- ► There are more variations among our manuscripts than there are words in the New Testament. (p. 90)

- ► We don't even have copies of the copies of the originals, or copies of the copies of the copies of the originals. What we have are copies made later—much later. In most instances, they are copies made many centuries later. And these copies all differ from one another, in many thousands of places. (p. 10, emphasis in the original)

- ► In the early Christian centuries, scribes were amateurs and as such were more inclined to alter the texts they copied... (p. 98)

- ► This was a human book from beginning to end. (p. 11)

These statements are either outright false or misleading at best. To an audience that is congenial to any propaganda that attacks the Bible, these words are swallowed uncritically, and Ehrman is championed as something of a "leading authority." This lesson contains a partial response. For a more complete countermeasure to these ideas, see the books mentioned in the "Helpful References" section at the end of this chapter—especially Edward D. Andrews' *Misrepresenting Jesus: Debunking Bart D. Ehrman's "Misquoting Jesus."*

ΛΘ

ΤΗ ΨΥΧΗ ΟΜΟΥ ΤΟΝ ΕΑΥΤΩΝ ΤΡΑ
ΧΗΛΟΝ ΥΠΕΘΗΚΑΝ ΟΙΣ ΟΥΚ ΕΓΩ ΜΟ
ΝΟΣ ΕΥΧΑΡΙΣΤΩ ΑΛΛΑ ΚΑΙ ΠΑΣΑΙ ΑΙ ΕΚ
ΚΛΗΣΙΑΙ ΤΩΝ ΕΘΝΩΝ ΚΑΙ ΤΗΝ ΚΑΤ ΟΙ
ΚΟΝ ΑΥΤΩΝ ΕΚΚΛΗΣΙΑΝ ΑΣΠΑΣΑΣΘΕ
ΕΠΑΙΝΕΤΟΝ ΤΟΝ ΑΓΑΠΗΤΟΝ ΜΟΥ ΟΥ
ΕΣΤΙΝ ΑΠΑΡΧΗ ΤΗΣ ΑΣΙΑΣ ΕΙΣ ΧΝ
ΑΣΠΑΣΑΣΘΕ ΜΑΡΙΑΝ ΗΤΙΣ ΠΟΛΛΑ ΕΚΟ
ΠΙΑΣΕΝ ΕΙΣ ΥΜΑΣ ΑΣΠΑΣΑΣΘΕ ΑΝΔΡΟ
ΝΕΙΚΟΝ ΚΑΙ ΙΟΥΛΙΑΝ ΤΟΥΣ ΣΥΝΓΕΝΕΙΣ ΜΟΥ
ΚΑΙ ΤΟΥΣ ΣΥΝΑΙΧΜΑΛΩΤΟΥΣ ΜΟΥ ΟΙΤΙΝΕΣ
ΕΙΣΙΝ ΕΠΙΣΗΜΟΙ ΕΝ ΤΟΙΣ ΑΠΟΣΤΟΛΟΙΣ ΟΙ
ΚΑΙ ΠΡΟ ΕΜΟΥ ΓΕΓΟΝΕΝ ΕΝ ΧΡΩ ΑΣΠΑ
ΟΕΣΘΩ ΠΑΛΙΑ ΤΟΝ ΤΟΝ ΑΓΑΠΗΤΟΝ ΕΝ ΚΩ
ΑΣΠΑΣΑΣΘΕ ΟΥΡΒΑΝΟΝ ΤΟΝ ΣΥΝΕΡΓΟΝ
ΗΜΩΝ ΕΝ ΧΡΩ ΚΑΙ ΣΤΑΧΥΝ ΤΟΝ ΑΓΑΠΗ
ΤΟΝ ΜΟΥ ΑΣΠΑΣΑΣΘΕ ΑΠΕΛΛΗΝ ΤΟΝ ΔΟΚΙ
ΜΟΝ ΕΝ ΧΡΩ ΑΣΠΑΣΑΣΘΕ ΤΟΥΣ ΕΚ ΤΩΝ
ΑΡΙΣΤΟΒΟΥΛΟΥ ΑΣΠΑΣΑΣΘΕ ΗΡΩΔΙΩΝΑ

Honestly Assessing the Evidence

In spite of Ehrman's skepticism, there is actually sound reason for confidence in the integrity of the transmission process for New Testament manuscripts. The following points are a summary of the evidence:

opposite page
Papyrus leaf of P46 (and Romans 16) dating from c. A.D. 200 or earlier

- We admittedly do not have any original documents of New Testament books autographed by the apostles themselves, but there are approximately 5,800 Greek manuscript copies of portions of the text (and, in some cases, entire books).

- Compare this to other ancient works of literature:
  - Virgil (70–19 B.C.)—5 manuscripts
  - Josephus (A.D. 37–100)—9 complete manuscripts
  - Tacitus (A.D. 59–129)—33 manuscripts
  - Julius Caesar's Gallic Wars (51–46 B.C.)—251 manuscripts dating between the ninth and 15th centuries

- Of the 5,800 Greek N.T. manuscripts in existence, over 100 papyri date from the second and third centuries. Some were copied within just a few decades of the original published documents!

- The New Testament, then, is by far the best-documented work of its kind in the entire world! No doubt there were thousands more that have not survived the rigors of decay or the flames of persecution.

- Most of the textual variants (discrepancies) involve minor issues such as word order, spelling, insignificant word variation, or conflation with a parallel account (especially common with Gospels). In some cases an over-zealous scribe sought to "correct" a perceived mistake in the manuscript from which he was copying.

- Both Philip Comfort and Edward Andrews, in the works cited below, make a strong case based on the physical evidence that the scribes in the earliest centuries were more faithful to their task than scribes of a later period.

- There is a question as to how to count the various discrepancies. The entire New Testament contains 138,020 words, but only "364 variants (1,092 words by our average) with which we have difficulty, a mere 10 of which involve great difficulty in deciding which reading to put in the text. Our average would make these variants 0.791 percent of the text..." (Andrews, p. 346).

A Perceived Weakness Is Actually a Strength

But why, in a matter so important, would God allow any variations or human mistakes in the transmission of the text? Would not even a single scribal miscue taint the whole process and compromise our faith in the Word of God? How can we have confidence in what the original documents would have said? What unbelievers interpret as a weakness is actually strength in disguise, illustrating once again that God's ways are not man's ways, and that God's wisdom "surprises" man's foolishness.

In much the same way that independent "local churches" spread over a wide area have advantages over a central bureaucracy, the dispersion of imperfect hand-copied manuscripts, distributed over a wide area, actually increases confidence in the original exemplars.

- ▶ With thousands of copies (in some cases not too many generations removed from the originals), there is less tendency to "idolize" a single manuscript.

- ▶ Enemies of the truth are not able to cast doubt on the whole message by discrediting just one document.

- ▶ Just as eyewitness divergence strengthens the case of overlapping testimony, manuscript divergence enhances what they testify in common—which is essentially 99% of the message (with the remaining 1% not threatening any fundamental teaching).

- ▶ Destroy or burn one, and the core message will not be affected. There are still nearly 6,000 others in existence all over the world.

- ▶ Just as independent local churches, even with their imperfections and non-essential differences, are living examples of the same original blueprint, the surviving manuscripts point backward to an original that can be reconstructed with a high degree of confidence.

- ▶ Most of the divergences (manuscript variations) are readily identifiable as human mistakes, countered by the prevalence of uniform witnesses which are more trustworthy.

- ▶ The four or five different "manuscript families" show that when one early mistake was transcribed onto a manuscript that came to be trusted as a "parent copy" in a given region, scribes generally tried to faithfully reproduce their

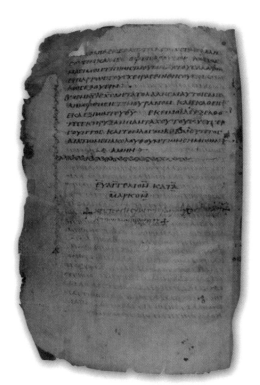

The end of Mark, Codex Washingtonianus, c. A.D. 400. This copy of Mark's Gospel has a variant ending unique to itself.

"best witness" to the original text—which underscores the
general reliability of the entire transmission process.

Codex Vaticanus, one of the oldest and best witnesses of a nearly complete Bible

In the Final Analysis...

Interestingly enough, Bart Ehrman's mentor was world-renowned
textual scholar, Bruce Metzger, who had a much healthier view of
the integrity of the biblical text than Ehrman does. Yet Ehrman
says of Metzger,

An eighth-century scribe on the laborious nature of the task:

> Oh, you lucky reader, before you touch a book wash your hands, turn the pages carefully and keep your fingers well away from the letters! For someone unable to write cannot imagine what an immense labor it is. Oh how hard is writing: it blurs the eyes, squeezes the kidneys, and tortures every limb. Only three fingers write, but the whole body suffers…

I have nothing but respect and admiration for him. In addition, even though we may disagree on important religious questions—he is a firmly committed Christian and I am not—we are in complete agreement on a number of very important historical and textual questions. If he and I were put in a room and asked to hammer out a consensus statement on what we think the original text of the New Testament probably looked like, there would be very few points of disagreement—maybe one or two dozen places out of many thousands (*Misquoting Jesus*, p. 252).

If the preceding statement is taken at face value, then even one of the world's leading biblical skeptics is admitting, in a moment of honesty, that the original New Testament text can be fundamentally reconstructed with near-100% accuracy.

The highly respected scholar, Sir Frederic Kenyon, summarized the textual evidence this way:

> The interval then between the dates of original composition and the earliest extant evidence becomes so small as to be in fact negligible, and the last foundation for any doubt that the Scriptures have come down to us substantially as they were written has now been removed. Both the authenticity and the general integrity of the books of the New Testament may be regarded as finally established (*The Bible and Archaeology* [New York: Harper, 1940], pp. 288–289).

Questions

1. Summarize the perceived weakness in the transmission of the sacred text.

2. What is the actual state of the manuscript evidence?

3. In what ways is the perceived weakness actually a strength in disguise?

Helpful References

Edward D. Andrews. *Misrepresenting Jesus: Debunking Bart D. Ehrman's "Misquoting Jesus."* 3rd ed. Cambridge, OH: Christian Publishing House, 2017.

F. F. Bruce, *The New Testament Documents: Are They Reliable?* Grand Rapids, MI: Eerdmans, 1950.

Martin Luther New Testament page, 1534

LESSON 8
Scribal Practices of Early Christians

Examining the Material Evidence

We can learn much about the transmission of the biblical manuscripts from a careful examination of material evidence. Here are a few examples.

- When the scribe used parchment, the manuscript had pinpricks placed in it, so that it could be ruled by lines to mark the horizontal and vertical boundaries.

- In some manuscripts the lines are still faintly visible. In many documents, there are a consistent number of lines per page.

- Early Christians had a decided preference for the "codex" book form versus the scroll. According to one count, Christian codices account for somewhere between 22 to 34% of the total documents for the second and third centuries, yet Christian books amount to only about 2% (codices and rolls).

- Over 95% of Christian copies of the Old Testament writings are in codex form, whereas Jews tended to prefer scrolls—and the same goes for virtually 100% of the extant New Testament writings.

- So far, 127 New Testament manuscripts, including many from the second, third, and fourth centuries, have been discovered that were written on papyrus. The majority were produced on parchment or vellum (leather skin), especially from the fourth century on.

- In some cases, there is a little artwork, such as some scribal designs at the end of each Gospel in the Codex Washingtonianus.

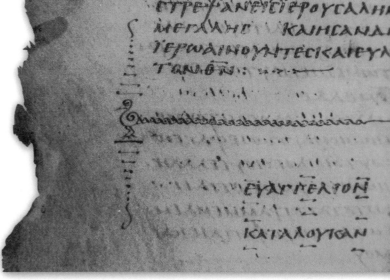

Each Gospel in Codex W ends with design-work as in this last page of Luke. Scribal doodles, personal signature, or guild trademark? Does the bird on the left have special significance?

▶ In the Codex Sinaiticus, some red ink headings signaling male and female speakers are differentiated from the brown ink of the sacred text in the Song of Solomon.

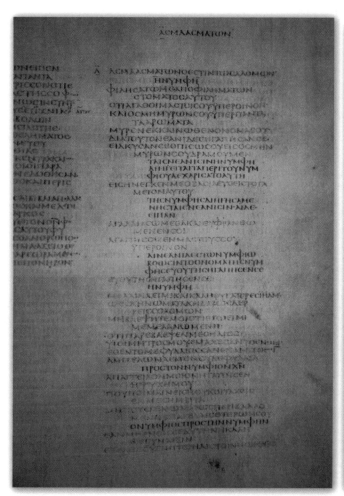

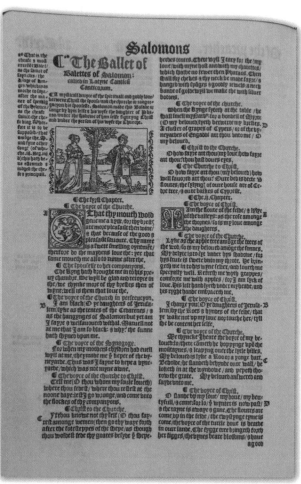

Song of Solomon in the Sinaiticus on the left…and with a similar "red ink" format in the "Matthew" Bible, 1537, on the right

Scriptoria

A scriptorium was a room where scribes worked to produce manuscripts. A lector would read the exemplar, and one or more scribes would write down his words. A master scribe or foreman would then make needed corrections. In some of the manuscript copies, we can actually see where corrections were made. Many of the earliest manuscripts were, in fact, written by professional scribes or by copyists skilled in preparing documents. In the middle ages, some monasteries served as centers for copying Scripture by hand. In the earliest centuries of the church, there were prominent scriptoria in places like Alexandria, Egypt—the region where some of the best and earliest copies were preserved.

Sacred Names (Latin: *Nomina Sacra*)

One of the most fascinating and instructive facets of the transmission of the sacred text has to do with how scribes communicated sacred names. In the Old Testament, one name carried special significance—YHWH. Sometimes called the "Tetragrammaton," i.e. the four-letter word, YHWH is often spelled Yahweh or Jehovah.

This was God's personal "covenant" name to the Israelites. Related to the Hebrew verb "to be," YHWH carried the idea of eternal self-existence. When Moses asked for God's name, the Lord told him to tell the Israelites that "I AM" had commissioned him (Ex 3:6, 13–15). God's holy name was never to be desecrated. A half Egyptian "blasphemed the Name and cursed" (Lev 24:11). The offender was stoned to death.

In a later development, the Israelites came to substitute the term *Adonai* (pronounced a-dough-NIGH) or "my Lord," for YHWH when reading the text. Consequently, several modern English versions honor this tradition by translating YHWH with the capital letters, LORD.

In the third century B.C., the Old Testament scriptures were translated into Greek. The version is called the *Septuagint*, which means "seventy" (after an old tradition of 70 translators, and abbreviated with the Roman numerals LXX). For a while, at least, Jewish scribes put the Hebrew letters "YHWH" even in a Greek text when writing out the sacred Name. Eventually, the Greek word for "Lord" (Kurios) was used.

יהוה	YHWH, Yahweh (Jehovah)	κύριος	Lord
	(Hebrew)		(Greek)

Christians, like Jews before them, tried to avoid idolatrous images in their art. Certain forms became somewhat standardized early on. There was the sign of the "fish," from the Greek ICHTHYS, which forms an acrostic symbol for "Jesus Christ, Son of God, Savior." Sometimes, Jesus is depicted as the Good Shepherd (John 10). Also popular was the Chi-Rho symbol, representing the first two letters of CHRISTOS, or Christ. (The two letters look like an X and a P in English script). This was often written with the Greek letters, alpha and omega, to the left and right of the Chi-Rho.

A Christian's gravestone, Cologne, Germany

Closeup of the Chi-Rho (cross) symbol, with Alpha and Omega

In early Christian documents, especially manuscripts of the New Testament, there was also a way of preserving sacred names, called *nomina sacra*:

Term	Greek Word		Abbreviation	
Lord	Kurios	Κύριος	KS	K̄Σ̄
God	Theos	Θεός	THS	Θ̄Σ̄
Jesus	Iēsous	Ἰησοῦς	IE or IES	ĪH̄Σ̄ or ĪΣ̄
Christ	Christos	Χριστός	CHR or CHS	X̄P̄ or X̄Σ̄
Spirit	Pneuma	Πνεῦμα	PNA	Π̄N̄Ā
Cross	Stauros	Σταυρός	S-ΡΩS (written with a staurogram, a P with a cross)	⳨
Crucify	Stauromai	Σταυρόμαι	S-ΡΩMAI (written with a staurogram, a P with a cross)	⳨

The names were suspended or contracted, and the scribes placed a horizontal bar over the name as a context clue of its holy significance.

Interestingly enough, the forms were standardized early on—possibly as early as the first century. The key *nomina sacra* abbreviations are in all the early manuscripts, including the earliest ones. Ironically, when "lord," "god," or "spirit" are not to be intended as sacred names, then the Greek word is spelled out in full. One example is 1 Cor 8:5–6, where I have emphasized only the abbreviated sacred names in the Greek manuscripts—"For although there may be so-called gods in heaven or on earth—as indeed there are many 'gods' and many 'lords'—yet for us there is one God, the Father, from whom are all things and for whom we exist, and one Lord, Jesus Christ, through whom are all things and through whom we exist."

In fact, scholars know when an ancient Greek manuscript of the Old Testament was produced by a Christian or Jewish scribe simply by the presence (or absence) of these "nomina sacra" designations.

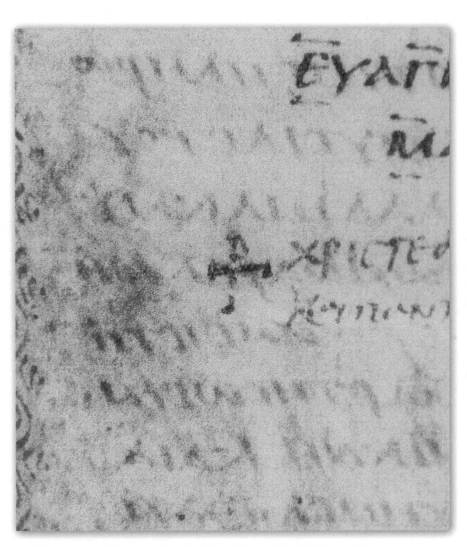

Can you see the cross sign in this ending of Mark's Gospel?

Codex Sinaiticus (1 Cor. 8): many "gods" and "lords" (spelled out in full)…but one "Lord Jesus Christ" (all abbreviated as sacred)

Lessons

1. For Christians, there is God the Father, God the Son, and God the Holy Spirit (1 Cor 8:5–6; Eph 4:4–6).

2. Christians should guard their tongues when using "sacred names." Jews held in high esteem the sacred name, YHWH, and early Christian practice was to show the same respect for Jesus and the Holy Spirit. Should the "name which is above every name" ever be used in a careless or derogatory manner? Phil 2:9–11

3. Since this "system" was standardized very early on, it gives us additional confidence in the faithful transmission of the sacred text. I.e. scribes followed certain procedures from ancient times, and this is a peculiar, but powerful testimony to the integrity of the transmission process. Scribes were not to "add" or "take away" (Rev 22:18–19), and this applied even to the special representation of significant nouns.

4. Readers ("lectors") understood the codes (Rev. 1:3). There probably was special emphasis or pronunciation given to the sacred names.

5. Even "cross" carries special significance (1 Cor 1:18–24). An object of ridicule to pagans, the "cross of Christ" was a badge of honor to Christians, even to the point of treating the word *cross* as a sacred name.

First-century Roman graffiti making fun of Christians serving a crucified donkey: "Alexamenos worships his god." But to Christians, a crucified Savior, which was "folly to those who are perishing," was, in fact, testimony to the power and wisdom of God (1 Cor 1:18–24).

Helpful References

Philip W. Comfort, *Encountering the Manuscripts: An Introduction to New Testament Paleography and Textual Criticism*. Nashville, TN: Broadman & Holman, 2005.

Edward D. Andrews. *Misrepresenting Jesus: Debunking Bart D. Ehrman's "Misquoting Jesus."* 3rd ed. Cambridge, OH: Christian Publishing House, 2017.

First-century Roman graffiti scratched in plaster on the wall of a room. Housed in the Palatine Hill Museum in Rome.

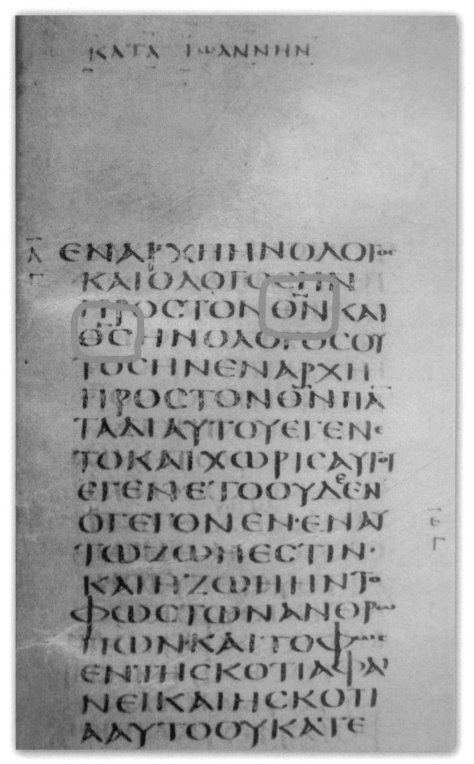

John 1:1 in the Codex Sinaiticus. Was "the Word" just "a god" or "God"? Can you see the answer for yourself in the text?

LESSON 9
Witnesses to the Original Text: The Hard Evidence

Greek and Hebrew Manuscripts

The primary witnesses to the original text of the Bible are manuscripts in the original languages. We have addressed the Hebrew manuscripts for the Old Testament and the Greek manuscripts for the New Testament. Once housed in scriptoria, synagogues, and monasteries, they are now largely found in museums across the world. There are various tools to help students assess the manuscript evidence (and possible textual variants) for each verse of the Bible. For example, I have personally found the following tools to be quite beneficial:

- Annotated editions of the Hebrew Bible (Tanakh), such as *Biblia Hebraica Stuttgartensia* (BHS), or the Greek New Testament, such as the United Bible Societies (UBS) or Nestle-Aland (NA) editions of the text

- Bruce M. Metzger, *A Textual Commentary of the Greek New Testament*

- Philip W. Comfort, *New Testament Text and Translation Commentary*

In general, however, the overall testimony of these manuscripts is decisive, if not overwhelming. In only a relative few cases are there major questions about what the original text would have said, and none of these instances threatens a single biblical teaching.

The Isaiah scroll found among the Dead Sea Scrolls in 1947 was about 1,000 years older than any other Hebrew manuscript of Isaiah at the time. This scroll may be as early as the second century B.C., and the portion above includes one of the greatest Messianic prophecies—Isaiah 53.

The Dead Sea Scrolls

Discovery of the Dead Sea Scrolls in 1947 electrified the world and became one of the great archaeological events of the 20th century. Eventually this included a collection of thousands of fragments comprising around 900 scrolls. They date from about 250 B.C. to A.D. 68 and include about 207 biblical manuscripts, with some Hebrew texts about 1,000 years older than the next oldest copies.

They also involve commentaries on biblical books and a Community Rule, also known as the "Manual of Discipline." The Dead Sea Scrolls community, thought by many to be Essenes, was very covenant-oriented. Much can be learned from these documents about their understanding of concepts related to the New Covenant (Jer 31:31–34), as well as Jewish backgrounds in the first-century world of the New Testament.

A personal favorite edition of the Dead Sea Scrolls (published in 1967), by Geza Vermes and Heritage Press, with illustrations by Shraga Weil.

Citations of Early Christians

Early Christians and "church fathers" in the first four centuries of the church cite virtually the entire New Testament and much of the Old Testament in their writings. This evidence corroborates that found in the primary manuscripts. If there is an early textual variant, scholars can even isolate the "manuscript family" of the text being cited by an ancient Christian.

Early Translations

In the third century B.C., Jewish scholars undertook a prominent translation of the Hebrew Old Testament into the Greek language. This is now known as the Septuagint translation. It stands as an independent witness to the Old Testament, along with the Masoretic Hebrew text. Sometimes the New Testament writers themselves, writing in Greek, cite the Septuagint version instead of the Hebrew text. Early Christians, many of whom spoke Greek, used it widely, and it is found in the Codex Sinaiticus and other collections used by Christians.

With the rapid spread of the gospel, there was a need to translate the Scriptures into other languages. Consequently, there are early translations of the Bible into Latin, Syriac, Ethiopic, Gothic, Armenian, Arabic, and other languages. These are further independent witnesses to the original text.

Syriac Peshitta

Even though there was an earlier Latin version, Jerome undertook a new translation of the Bible into the Latin at the end of the fourth century. The Latin "Vulgate" (or "common" version) became the standard Bible of the western medieval world and the Roman Catholic Church.

Page from the Lindisfarne Gospels, c. A.D. 715, Latin Vulgate

Summing Up—A Wealth of Evidence

Since we have multiple independent witnesses to the original text of the Bible, in multiple languages, in thousands of manuscripts, discovered in diverse regions, the cumulative evidence for the original text is somewhat overwhelming. There may be legitimate questions raised about the textual integrity of a few passages, but for the Bible as a whole the case is quite strong. Scholars have reconstructed a "master text" that eliminates the vast majority of scribal mistakes. Why is "human error" not an issue for over 99% of the text? As Edward Andrews says, "We know what the original reading is with absolute certainty."

Bonus Material—What about the Apocrypha?

The term *Apocrypha* usually refers to a group of Jewish books written during the intertestamental period (between the Old Testament and New Testament). There are also apocryphal books identified with New Testament figures, written in subsequent centuries. The term literally means "hidden," and the secret lore of these books was often judged, rightly so, as heretical.

The books in question had long been considered outside the biblical canon (see Lesson 5). Even the Latin Vulgate of the late fourth century did not include them. The translator Jerome made clear in his prologue that the Apocryphal books might be edifying, but were not canonical. Their inclusion in some Bibles, especially Roman Catholic Bibles, has a curious history. At the dawn of the Protestant Reformation, Martin Luther, William Tyndale, and other reformers saw the Bible as the sole authority in matters of belief and practice. Luther gathered the "outside books" from Greek and Latin manuscripts and placed them in a separate section between the two testaments of his 1534 German translation under the heading, "Apocrypha." They were not on the same level as the canonical Scriptures but were "useful and good for reading."

Apocrypha contents page in a Luther Bible: "not held equal to Holy Scripture" but "useful and good for reading."

The Roman Catholic Church retaliated at the Council of Trent in 1546 by honoring all the Apocrypha except 1–2 Esdras and the Prayer of Manasseh. Instead of speaking of these books as apocryphal, Catholics prefer to call them "deuterocanonical," to indicate that their status was settled later than that of the "proto-canonical" books.

In the English-speaking world, William Tyndale did not translate or include the apocryphal books as Scripture, but subsequent editions of the Bible in England pandered to the monarch, as head of the Anglican Church, which was the most "Catholic" of all the Protestant groups. Consequently, many early Bibles in England are arranged with the following sections:

1. The Anglican "Book of Common Prayer"

2. The Old Testament

3. The Apocrypha

4. The New Testament

5. Metrical Psalms (essentially their hymnal).

The apocryphal books themselves are a hodgepodge of intertestamental histories, romance novels, moral instruction, and fictitious elaboration on persons or events from the Old Testament. The book of 1 Maccabees is a fairly credible historical work covering the period from 175 to 134 B.C. and focusing on Jews winning independence from the foreign ruler, Antiochus IV. Some of these events are prophesied in the book of Daniel, and they gave rise to the Jewish celebration of Hanukkah. On the other hand, *Bel and the Dragon*, *The Prayer of Azariah and the Song of the Three Holy Children*, and *Susanna* are fictitious additions to the book of Daniel. *The Letter of Jeremiah* purports to be a letter from the biblical prophet to Jews who were about to be taken into exile. Tobit is a fictitious romance novel of life in Assyrian captivity. These and other apocryphal books are vastly inferior to the genuine biblical books. Their primary value lies in what they can tell us about Jewish literary tendencies a few centuries prior to the New Testament era.

A Geneva Bible with Apocrypha, 1607

The Talmud, the first-century Jewish historian Josephus, and the New Testament (Luke 24:44) all recognize the ancient three-fold division of the Old Testament which consists of the same 39 books we now possess (although some, such as 1–2 Samuel and 1–2 Kings were combined into one "book" in the ancient lists). Even one of the apocryphal books alludes to this threefold grouping. The Wisdom of Jesus Ben-Sirach (a.k.a. *Ecclesiasticus*, dated 132 B.C.) has a forward or prologue which says,

> *The Law, the Prophets, and the Latter Writers* have left us a wealth of valuable teachings... That is why my grandfather Jesus devoted himself to reading *the Law, the Prophets, and the Other Books* of our ancestors. After he had mastered them, he was led to write a book of his own. (emphasis added)

Obviously, this apocryphal book was intended to be an addition to the books that were already formally recognized as a sacred collection—a corpus of writings we now call the Old Testament (see Lesson 6). Furthermore, 1 Maccabees speaks of a "time of great trouble for Israel, worse than anything that had happened to them since *the time prophets ceased to appear among them*" (9:27, emphasis added). The people longed for a "true prophet" (4:46; 14:41), but they would have to wait for John the Baptist.

The modern Christian has these and many other good reasons for rejecting the Apocrypha as non-canonical and reverently accepting the 66 "received" books commonly included in the Holy Bible.

Questions

1. What is the biblical rule concerning the testimony of witnesses? Deut 19:15

2. Are there at least two or three independent witnesses to the biblical text? List some examples cited in the lesson.

3. Even with a slight degree of divergence (which rules out collusion), these witnesses largely agree. What should we conclude from this evidence?

4. Should the apocryphal books be included in our Bibles? Why or why not?

Helpful References

Edward D. Andrews. Misrepresenting Jesus: Debunking Bart D. Ehrman's "Misquoting Jesus." 3rd ed. Cambridge, OH: Christian Publishing House, 2017.

Philip Comfort, ed., *The Origin of the Bible.* Wheaton, IL: Tyndale House, 2003.

Reader's Digest, *The Bible Through the Ages.* Pleasantville, NY: Reader's Digest Association, 1996.

Géza Vermès, *The Dead Sea Scrolls in English.* New York: Heritage Press, 1962.

Israel Antiquities Authority, *Dead Sea Scrolls: Life and Faith in Biblical Times.* New York: Ralph Appelbaum Associates, 2012.

Medieval walls of Rothenburg, Germany

LESSON 10
Holy Scripture in the Middle Ages

The medieval Cathedral in Cologne, Germany

The medieval period was truly the "Dark Ages" of biblical literacy for the masses, in spite of Europe being a so-called "Christian" society. The Bible was copied, studied, and hidden in various monasteries, but the common people received a "filtered" version. David Daniell summarizes the situation:

> For the medieval Church, the Bible certainly had authority, but it was alongside the greater authority of the practices and traditions which had grown over the centuries [in Roman Catholicism]... In the teaching and preaching of the Church, the Bible, in Latin, was a sacred text from which verses, or

The Irish Book of Kells

Can you read the Latin? Neither could early speakers of English!
This manuscript is obviously stunningly beautiful,
but not intended as a Bible for common people.

illustrative incidents, could be extracted and used to underpin the common people's proper attention to the liturgies. The whole Bible was not in the picture. (*The Bible in English*, p. xix)

All this changed in the 14th century when John Wycliffe spearheaded a new English Bible translation, although not without significant resistance from ecclesiastical authorities. An opponent of John Wycliffe in the early 15th century complained that "the pearl of the gospel" that "Christ gave to the doctors and clergy of the Church" was being "scattered abroad and trodden underfoot by swine." It was argued the common people had no need of the Bible. After all, they had stained glass windows in the cathedrals, biblical scenes painted on walls, and plays depicting scriptural stories. Looking back on this period, we admire Romanesque and Gothic architecture, colorful manuscript art, the huge castles, knights in shining armor, and other vestiges of medieval society, but the repression of biblical truth was a tragic reality.

Book of Hours, Use of Rome, 1505

The Catholic Church miscalculated its self-assumed caretaker role and played an evil bureaucratic power game. The tactic backfired. The reformers, on the other hand, tapped into an intense spiritual hunger at the grassroots level when they exposed the Church's corruption and accused senior clergy of locking up the Scriptures from the common folks. There would be no contagion of the fire that erupted all over Europe. People wanted to read the Bible as it was originally given—the Old Testament, the four Gospels, the Acts of the Apostles, the epistles, and the book of Revelation. In the early 14th century, Bishop Fitzralph of Armagh would say, "I used to think that I had penetrated to the depths of Your Truth with the citizens of Your Heaven; until You, the Solid Truth, shone upon me in Your Scriptures, scattering the cloud of my error, and showing me how I was croaking in the marshes with the toads and frogs."

The Furtmeyr Bible, German, late 15th century

Commissioned by a wealthy family pictured on the left

Vivid scenes from the Old Testament, the Virgin Mary

Scenes from Exodus, Furtmeyr Bible

When scholars associated with Wycliffe translated the Scriptures from the Latin Vulgate into "middle English" in the 1380s, the manuscripts were painstakingly handwritten, as the printing press would not produce a Latin Vulgate until 1455 or a Tyndale New Testament until 1526. In spite of intense efforts to ban them, burn them, and burn those who read them, copies of the Wycliffe Bibles were abundant. About 20 manuscripts of the whole Bible still survive, and almost 90 of the entire New Testament—over 250 in all, including single books. This is a larger number of copies than for any other medieval English text.

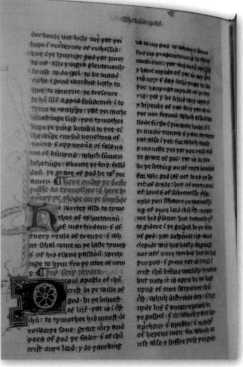

The Wycliffe New Testament

Moreover, as David Daniell observes, these Wycliffe Bibles came "with obvious care, written on vellum to last," and "generally free from additional matter." Moreover, they contained "nothing to identify the translator, the place of origin or date." The silence is noteworthy. The focus would be on the sacred text.

John Wycliffe (1330–1384)

Wycliffe launched a movement that could not be extinguished, and he is remembered as the "Morning Star" of the Reformation. However, the Catholic Church tried hard to destroy his work and discredit him. Under the influence of Archbishop Arundel, a 1407 ruling forbade the translation of "any text of Holy Scripture into the English or other language, by way of book, pamphlet, or tract, and that no book, pamphlet or tract of this kind be read, either recently composed at the time of the said John Wycliffe, or since then, or that in future may be composed…under pain of the greater excommunication…" To add insult to injury, Wycliffe's body was exhumed 44 years after his death, his remains were burned, and the ashes were scattered over the river Swift.

There were persecutions and even inquisitions intended to stamp out dissent, but they had the opposite effect. An Englishman of the time complained that "a man could not meet two people on the road, but one of them was a disciple of Wycliffe." Wycliffe's writings were banned and burned in England, but they caught on in Bohemia, where Jan Hus would launch a pre-Reformation, "back to the Bible" movement of his own.

Even in 15th century England, a group of people called "Lollards" (derogatory for "ranters") took up Wycliffe's cause. They thought of themselves as a network of "true Christians." Their prevailing assumptions were reinforced by itinerant "poor preachers," tracts, and portions of the Wycliffe Bible, covertly shared. Many attended the Catholic mass as well as their own illegal "conventicles" (assemblies). Their meetings, often late into the night, focused on memorizing Scripture in their native English. In general, through a simple study of the Bible, many Lollards came to the following conclusions:

- ▶ Images were not to be worshiped.
- ▶ Elaborate and costly church buildings were not holy.
- ▶ God commanded no holy days or fast days but Sunday.
- ▶ The Roman Catholic Church was rich and corrupt.
- ▶ Confession to a priest was a human invention.
- ▶ Holy bread and water are unauthorized.
- ▶ The pope was the antichrist.
- ▶ Christians should not pray for the dead.
- ▶ Infant baptism is foreign to Scripture.
- ▶ Musical instruments should not be used in the musical praise of the church.

Wycliffe's bones are exhumed, burned, and cast into a stream

Woodcut from John Foxe's *Acts and Monuments*

Access to the Bible changed the equation forever. For a time, the Roman Catholic authorities would suppress dissent, but they were simply coiling a spring so tight that it erupted with explosive force in the 16th century.

Questions

1. Some have argued that many people in the Middle Ages were ignorant and could not read, but that the access they had to the Bible, even in different formats, served them well. For example, a popular venue was the mystery play, in which biblical scenes were acted out. In what ways does this argument fall short?

2. From the proliferation of hand-copied portions of the Wycliffe Bible (and a century-and-a-half later by the printed Tyndale pocket-sized New Testament), it is obvious there was pent-up demand for the Bible. People smuggled contraband copies and risked their lives in possessing and reading them. In what ways do we have an opposite problem today

3. The early Reformers were convinced of the power of God's Word to change people as well as the larger society (cf. Rom 1:16; Heb 4:12; 1 Thess 2:13). How can we recapture this faith in God's Word in a postmodern age in which the Bible is often scorned and ridiculed?

4. What are some advantages to possessing a complete copy of the Old and New Testaments? 2 Tim 2:15; 3:16–17; Ps 119:105

Helpful References

David Daniell, *The Bible in English: Its History and Influence*. New Haven: Yale University Press, 2003.

Lori Anne Ferrell, *The Bible and the People*. New Haven: Yale University Press, 2008.

Michael Frassetto, *The Great Medieval Heretics: Five Centuries of Religious Dissent*. New York: BlueBridge, 2008.

Felipe Fernández-Armesto and Derek Wilson, *Reformations: A Radical Interpretation of Christianity and the World, 1500–2000*. New York: Scribner, 1997.

George Stokes, *Lives of the British Reformers: From Wickliff to Foxe*. New and rev. ed. London: The Religious Tract Society, 1873.

fuit: nūc aūt et michi ⁊ tibi vtilis: quē
remiſi tibi . Tu aūt illū ut mea viſcera
ſuſcipe. Quē ego voluerā mecū detine-
re: ut pro te michi miniſtraret ī vincu-
lis euāgelij. Sine cōſilio aūt tuo ni-
chil voluī facere: vtī ne velut ex neceſſi-
tate bonū tuū eſſet: ſed volūtariū . Foꝛ-
ſitan eī ideo diſceſſit ad horā a te: ut
eternū illū reciperes: iam nō ut ſeruum
ſed pro ſeruo cariſſimū frem: maxime
michi. Quāto aūt magis tibi: et ī car-
ne et ī dūo? Si ergo habes me ſociū:
ſuſcipe illū ſicut me. Si autē aliqd no-
cuit tibi aut debet: hoc michi imputa.
Ego paulus ſcripſi mea manu . Ego
reddam: ut non dicā tibi q̄ ⁊ teipm michi debes. Ita frater ego te fruar in do-
mino: refice viſcera mea ī criſto . Con-
fidens inobediētia tua ſcripſi tibi: ſciēs
qñi et ſup id q̄ð dico facies. Simul et
para michi hoſpiciū: nā ſpero p oratio-
nes vꝛas donari me vobis. Salutat
te epaftas ⁊ captiuus me⁹ in criſto iheſu: marc⁹ ariſtarchus demas ⁊ lucas
adiutores mei. Gratia dūi nꝛi iheſu
criſti cū ſpiritu veſtro amen . Jncipit
pꝛologus in. epłam. ad. hebreos.

In primis dicendū eſt cur apłus paulus ī hac epła ſcribendo nō ſeruauerit
moꝛem ſuū: ut vel vocabulū nominis
ſui vel oꝛdinis deſcriberet dignitatem.
Hec cauſa eſt q̄ ad eos ſcribēs q̄ ex cir-
cunciſione credideratt hi gentiū apo-
ſtolus ⁊ nō hebreoꝛ: ſciens quoꝗ eos
ſupbiam ſuāꝗ humilitate ipſe demō-
ſtꝛas meritū officij ſui noluit āteferre.
Na ſimili modo etiā iohānes apłus
propter humilitatē in epła ſua nomē
ſuū eadē ratone nō ꝑtulit. Hanc ergo
epłam fertur apoſtoł⁹ ad hebreos con-
ſcriptā hebraica lingua miſiſſe: cuius

ſeculum ⁊ oꝛdinē retinens lucas euan-
geliſta poſt exceſſum apoſtoli pauli
greco ſermone cōpoſuit. Jncipit epła.
ad hebreos. capitlm. primum. ꝗ

Multiphariē multiſꝗ
modis olim deus
loquēs patribus in
pꝛophetis: nouiſſi-
me diebꝫ iſtis locu-
tus ē nobis in filio
quē cōſtituit heredem vniuerſoꝛ: p quē
fecit et ſecła. Qui cū ſit ſplendoꝛ glorie:
et figura ſubſtātie eius · poꝛtanſꝗ oia
verbo virtutis ſue purgationē pecca-
toꝛū faciēs : ſedet ad dexterā maieſta-
tis in excelſis tanto melioꝛ angelis ef-
fedus: quanto differētius pre illis no-
men hereditauit. Cui eī dixit aliquādo angeloꝛ filius meus es tu ego ho-
die genui te? Et rurſum. Ego ero illi ī
patrem: ⁊ ipſe erit michi in filiū . Et cū
iterum introducit pꝛimogenitū in oꝛbē
terre dicit. Et adoꝛent eum omnes an-
geli dei . Et ad angelos quidem dicit.
Qui facit āgelos ſuos ſpiritus: et mi-
niſtros ſuos flammā ignis. Ad filiū
autem. Thronus tuus de⁹ in ſeculum
ſeculi: virga equitatis virga regni tui.
Dilexiſti iuſticiā et odiſti iniꝗtatem :
propterea vnxit te deus deus tuus o-
leo exultationis pre participibꝫ tuis.
Et tu in principio dūe terrā fundaſti:
et opera manuū tuarum ſunt celi. Jpſi
peribunt tu autē pmanebis: ⁊ omnes
ut veſtimentū veteraſcent . Et velut a-
mictum mutabis eos ⁊ mutabūtur:
tu autem idem ipſe es: ⁊ anni tui non
deficient. Ad quē aūt angeloꝛum dixit aliquādo ſede a dextris meis: quo-
aduſꝗ ponā inimicos tuos ſcabellū
pedū tuoꝛ? Mōne omnes⁹ ſūt āminiſtra-
torij ſpiritꝰ: ī miniſteriū miſſi propter

LESSON 11

Reform Movements and the Beginnings of Modern Translation

On April 4, 1519 in Coventry, England, six people were burned at the stake for teaching their children the "Lord's prayer" and the Ten Commandments in English. Several events, however, would spiral out of control, and within a generation the masses would have legal access to the Bible in their own language.

The Gutenberg Press

In some ways, an important event in the preceding century had already paved the way. With Johannes Gutenberg and the "printing press" revolution of the 15th century, hand-written manuscripts gave way to mass-produced printed books. In 1455, about 180 copies of Gutenberg's 42-line, Latin Vulgate Bible were printed. In 1999, the *A&E Network* ranked Gutenberg the #1 person of influence in the second millennium. Few people know of his personal dream for this new invention:

> God suffers in the multitude of souls whom His holy word cannot reach. Religious truth is imprisoned in a small number of manuscript books, which confine instead of spreading the public treasure. Let us break the seal which seals up holy things, and give wings to truth, in order that she may go and win every soul that comes into this world, by her word, no longer written at great expense by a hand easily palsied, but multiplied like the wind by an untiring machine.

> Yes, it is a press, certainly, but a press from which shall soon flow, in inexhaustible streams, the most abundant and most marvelous liquor that has ever flowed to relieve the thirst of men! Through it, God will spread His word. A spring of pure truth shall flow from it; like a new star it shall scatter the darkness of ignorance, and cause a light heretofore unknown to shine amongst men.

The Gutenberg Press

opposite page
The first chapter of Hebrews in a printed Gutenberg edition of the Latin Vulgate

Erasmus

Erasmus of Rotterdam was a prominent humanist and scholar who in the early 16th century produced an edition of the Greek text that Luther and Tyndale used in their famous translations. Theologically, he sought to reform the Roman Catholic Church, but only from the inside as a committed Catholic. A contemporary said, "Erasmus laid the egg that Luther hatched." Erasmus responded that he "expected quite another kind of bird."

 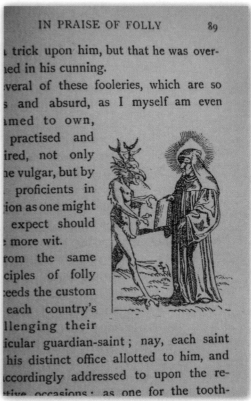

Erasmus's *In Praise of Folly* opened a door for the Reformation,
but Erasmus was too cautious to abandon the Catholic faith

On the other hand, he helped pave the way for the translations produced by the reformers. He said, "I totally dissent from those who are unwilling that the Sacred Scriptures, translated into the vulgar tongue, should be read by private individuals, as if Christ had taught such subtle doctrines that they can with difficulty be understood by a very few theologians, or as if the strength of the Christian religion lay in men's ignorance of it...Christ wishes

His mysteries to be published as widely as possible. I would even wish all women to read the gospel and the epistles of St. Paul."

He added, "And I wish they were translated into all the languages of all people, that they might be read and known, not merely by the Scotch and the Irish, but even by the Turks and the Saracens. I wish that the husbandman may sing parts of them at his plough, that the weaver may warble them at the shuttle, that the traveler may with their narratives beguile the weariness of the way."

The dream would be realized only by those who were willing to work *outside the system*.

Martin Luther

In an effort to fleece common people out of money that would finance St. Peter's Basilica in Rome, Johannes Tetzel sold indulgences: "As the coin in the coffer rings, so the soul from purgatory springs." Martin Luther called it "the pious defrauding of the faithful." As the conflict came to a head, on October 31, 1517, he nailed 95 theses for debate to the castle church door in Wittenberg, Germany.

Luther and the Wittenberg Castle Church made famous by the 95 theses posted in 1517

Pope Leo x moved to "quench a monk...Martin Luther by name, and thus smother the fire before it should become a conflagration." He called Luther a "wild boar" who had invaded "the Lord's vineyard." As events of the burgeoning Reformation played out, two divergent attitudes came to the forefront:

- ▸ On the one hand, Ignatius Loyola (founder of the Jesuit order) defended the powers that be: "I will believe that the white object I see is black if that should be the decision of the hierarchical church."
- ▸ On the other side was the defiant German monk: "A simple layman armed with Scripture is to be believed above a pope or a cardinal without it."—Martin Luther (Leipzig debate, June 1519)

Before the Holy Roman emperor, Charles V, and representatives from Rome, Luther confessed at the Diet of Worms in 1521:

> Unless I can be instructed and convinced with evidence from the Holy Scriptures…then I cannot and will not recant, because it is neither safe nor wise to act against conscience… Here I stand. I can do no other. So help me God. Amen.

For all the good that he did, Luther was a man of enigmas and contradictions. On the upside, he put the Bible back in the hands of the common people, translating the Bible into his native German. He also taught the priesthood of all believers and opened a door to religious freedom and the spirit of investigation. On the downside, he fought one theological extreme (Catholic meritorious "works") by going too far to the other ("faith alone"). He adamantly denied free will, and he retained many Catholic practices. In 1531 the Augsburg Confession solidified the "Lutheran Church"—the beginning of the first Protestant denomination.

William Tyndale

J. I. Mombert rightly says, "Tyndale's place in history has not yet been sufficiently recognized." Born around 1494 and executed for heresy in 1536, William Tyndale was the first to translate the entire New Testament from Greek into English and portions of the Old Testament from Hebrew into his native language. His editions were also the first printed Bibles in English.

Tyndale seems to have been heavily influenced by the Lollard movement (see Lesson 10). The first part of Mark 16:16 adorns the title page to his 1536 edition of the New Testament. He would argue for full immersion in baptism and say of Catholics, "They think that if the bishop butter the child in the forehead that it is safe."

After obtaining an education at Oxford (and possibly Cambridge as well), he began to gain a reputation as a preacher and independent thinker. On one occasion, a clergyman suggested, "We were better to be without God's law than the Pope's." Tyndale shot back: "I defy the Pope and all his laws, and if God spare my life ere many years, I will cause a boy that driveth the plow shall know more of the scripture than thou dost."

In explaining his burning desire to produce an English translation of the Bible, he said, "Because I had perceived by experience how that it was impossible to establish the lay people in any truth, except the scripture were plainly laid before their eyes in the mother tongue, that they might see the process, order, and meaning of the text"—i.e. the ability to see the entire sacred text in its original context.

William Tyndale (1494–1536)

In the mid-1520s, Bishop Cuthbert Tunstall of London, a friend of Erasmus, rejected Tyndale's plea for an English translation. In 1524, Tunstall warned all London printers against unapproved books, set up a board of censors, and issued the first license against imported books. Consequently, Tyndale left for Germany and the European continent. He would never return to his beloved England.

In Cologne, Germany, Tyndale's English translation began to materialize in 1525. After a spy discovered the plan and took sinister action, Tyndale and colleague William Roye had to escape up the Rhine to Worms with some of their manuscripts. The first printed English New Testament finally appeared in 1526. Justifying the need for an English Bible, Tyndale complained, "They have taken away the key of knowledge and beggared the people."

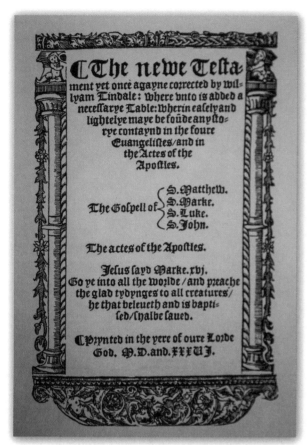

The 1536 Tyndale New Testament title page cites Mark 16:16

Tyndale's translation was brilliant. David Daniell says, "Part of his genius as a translator was his gift for knowing how ordinary people used language at slightly heightened moments and translating at that level." Tyndale introduced the following phrases into English:

- I am the light of the world
- So then faith cometh by hearing
- Let this cup pass from me
- Take, eat, this is my body
- Blessed are the poor in spirit
- God is love
- Psalms, hymns, and spiritual songs
- Work out your own salvation with fear and trembling
- I am not ashamed of the gospel
- Be strong in the Lord, and in the power of his might
- For thine is the kingdom and the power, and the glory forever

The impact of Tyndale's New Testament was immediate and profound, shedding light on an entirely new religious world. As David Teems suggests, "God had found a voice, and the voice was English." The little book could easily be tucked in a gown or a sleeve, and concealment was part of the charm of having one.

Tyndale's work gave new hope to the sinner. He said,

> And be the sinner never so weak, never so feeble and frail, sin he never so oft and so grievous, yet so long as this … mourning to be delivered remaineth in him, God seeth not his sins, reckoneth them not, for his truth's sake, and love to Christ. He is not a sinner in the sight of God that would be no sinner … His heart sinneth not, but mourneth, repenteth, and consenteth unto the

law and will of God, and justifieth God; that is, beareth record
that God which made the law is righteous and just.

—*The Parable of the Wicked Mammon*

Tyndale gave hope to common people. David Teems says,
"Tyndale's New Testament introduced a warm, generous, loving
God, a meddling God, a God truly interested in the affairs of ev-
eryday life, a God who cared for the neglected, those consigned
to the margins." David Ginsberg estimates that no one besides
Tyndale "saw fit to give the layman his due, to impress upon him
his personal relation to Scripture, i.e., that it was indeed for his
hands and eyes to hold and to interpret…he showed the pos-
sibility of a personal relationship with it." This was blasphemy to
Roman Catholicism—a threat to the old order.

The "Beast" of Revelation 13 in a Tyndale Bible (left) and Luther Bible (right)

Consequently, "Tyndale bashing" officially became vogue
among powerful enemies. David Daniell says this new version of
the New Testament was considered so dangerous "that it could
only be countered by the most vicious burnings, of books and

men and women." A bonfire was lit in London to burn the text, and Cardinal Lorenzo Campeggio proclaimed, "No holocaust could be more pleasing to God." According to one account, Bishop Tunstall purchased a heap of the Testaments in order to burn them, causing an outrage and also providing Tyndale some much-needed funds to keep his work going. Tyndale was not impressed:

> Finally, this threatening and forbidding the lay people to read the scripture is not for the love of your souls (which they care for as the fox doth for the geese)…

Part of the outrage of his opponents is that Tyndale's translation rightfully challenged some Catholic theological concepts by the use of the text itself. Here are some examples of words that have meaning in Tyndale's translation:

- "Congregation" (vs. "church")
- "Senior" (later "elder," presbyteros, vs. "priest")
- "Love" (vs. "charity")
- "Favor" (vs. "grace")
- "Acknowledge" (vs. "confess")
- "Repentance" (vs. "penance")

Tyndale became a hunted man. He revised the New Testament and began translating the Old Testament, as well as writing several books "on the run." Time ran out before he could complete the Old Testament, but he translated nearly half, and he preferred the Hebrew-English affinities to the Greek.

Secret agents were constantly frustrated by his stealth movements. For a time, Tyndale's concealment was greater than England's secret agents and bribes given to kidnap him. He was finally betrayed by Henry Phillips, arrested at Antwerp, imprisoned in Vilvorde Castle for 16 months, strangled to death, then burned at the stake. His final words were, "Lord, open the King of England's eyes."

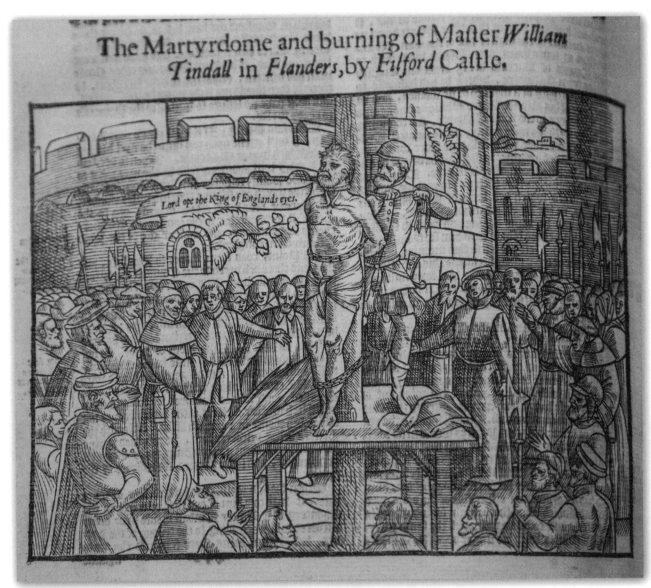

Woodcut of the martyrdom of William Tyndale in John Foxe's *Acts and Monuments*

Bonus Material: Tyndale in his own words...

Is the Roman Catholic Church the "true church"?

> They be all shameless to affirm that they be the right church and cannot err, though all the world seeth that not one of them is in the right way, and that they have with utter defiance forsaken both the doctrine and living of Christ and of all his apostles.
>
> —*An Answer to Sir Thomas More's Dialogue*

On Matt 16:18—

> Christ meant by the rock the confession that Peter had confessed... This faith is the rock whereon Christ's church is built... This faith is it, which saveth the congregation of Christ; and not Peter.
>
> —*Practice of the Prelates*

The first sentence of William Tyndale's preface to the New Testament (1536 edition):

> Here thou hast (most dear reader) the new testament or covenant made with us of God in Christ's blood.

Translation of Acts 2:38—

> **Wycliffe version:** And Peter said to them, Penance, he said, do ye, and each of you be baptized in the name of Jesus Christ, into remission of your sins; and ye shall take the gift of the Holy Ghost.

> **Tyndale version:** Peter said unto them: Repent and be baptized every one of you in the name of Jesus Christ, for the remission of sins, and ye shall receive the gift of the holy ghost.

On contemplating his own death (and commentary on Matt 5:10–12)—

> It is not enough to suffer for righteousness; but that no bitterness be left out of thy cup, thou shalt be reviled and railed upon; and even when thou art condemned to death, then be excommunicate and delivered to Satan, deprived of the fellowship of holy church, the company of angels, and of thy part in Christ's blood; and shalt be cursed down to hell, defied, detested, and execrate with all the blasphemous railings that the poisonful

heart of hypocrisies can think or imagine; and shalt see before thy face when thou goest to thy death, that all the world is persuaded and brought in belief that thou hast said and done that thou never thoughtest, and that thou diest for that thou art as guiltless of as the child that is unborn.

Well, though iniquity so highly prevail, and the truth for which thou diest, be so low kept under, and be not once known before the world, insomuch that it seemeth rather to be hindered by thy death than furthered, (which is of all griefs the greatest;) yet let not thine heart fail thee, neither despair, as though God had forsaken thee, or loved thee not; but comfort thyself with old ensamples, how God hath suffered all his old friends to be so entreated, and also his only and dear son Jesus; whose ensample, above all other, set before thine eyes, because thou art sure he was beloved above all other, that thou doubt not but thou art beloved also, and so much the more beloved, the more thou art like to the image of his ensample in suffering.

—Exposition of Matthew 5–7

Questions

1. What effect did the printing press have on the history of the Bible?

2. Erasmus was too cautious about leaving Roman Catholicism, even though he criticized some of its abuses and championed the right of the common people to have a translation in their native languages. Why do you suppose Luther and Tyndale had more long-term influence than Erasmus did?

3. What are some of the good things Luther accomplished?

4. What are some of the reasons Tyndale might be more influential to us than Luther was?

Helpful References

David Daniell, *The Bible in English: Its History and Influence*. New Haven: Yale University Press, 2003.

David Teems, *Tyndale: The Man Who Gave God an English Voice*. Nashville: Thomas Nelson, 2012.

Keith Sisman, *Traces of the Kingdom*. Rev. ed. Forbidden Books, 2011.

Banner of Truth, *Works of William Tyndale* (Parker Society).

Donald Smeeton, *Lollard Themes in the Reformation Theology of William Tyndale*. Kirksville, MO: Sixteenth Century Journal Publishers, 1986.

Luther's house in Wittenberg, Germany

LESSON 12
Bible Developments in English

After the death of William Tyndale, publication of the Bible in English began to escalate rather quickly. David Daniell estimates that from 1525 to 1640, printed English Bibles numbered over two million—and this for a population in England of only about six million. The popular demand was enormous!

However, as the English translation of Holy Scripture gained legal and societal acceptance, there was a downside. The powers-that-be hijacked the enterprise to their own ends. As Bibles in the English language gained mainstream status, the whole process of how the Bible was packaged reflected the "Church of England" bureaucracy or tributes to royal power. As persecution of dissenters eventually subsided in England, the radical commitment attached to owning a Bible also diminished, especially as many of the most committed separatists and dissenters headed for the New World. The eventual publication of the King James Version was a major accomplishment, but its biggest influence was felt across the Atlantic in America.

Matthew's Bible (1537)

In 1537 John Rogers assembled all of Tyndale's Bible translations and filled the remainder of the Old Testament books (Job to Malachi), as well as the Apocrypha, with Miles Coverdale's translations from the Latin, in a full-Bible English translation with royal approval. Thus, within a year after Tyndale's death, his dream and dying wish were fulfilled. At the foot of the title page are the words, "Set forth with the King's most gracious license." Since Tyndale's name was still

Matthew's Bible title page with reference to the "King's license"

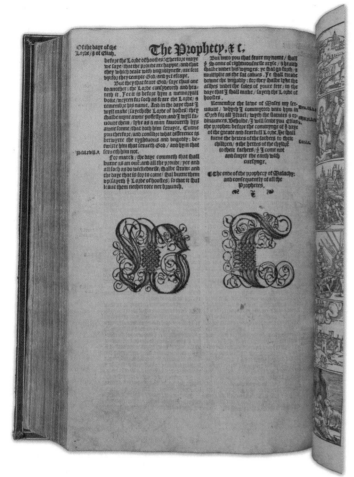

The Matthew's Bible gave cryptic tribute to William Tyndale (W. T.)

associated with heresy, Rogers used the names of two disciples—"translated into English by Thomas Matthew." 1,500 copies were printed in Antwerp, imported into England, and rapidly sold out. On the last page of the Old Testament are the heavily stylized initials, W. T., in a cryptic tribute to William Tyndale.

Later, John Rogers would become the first of almost 300 martyrs under Queen Mary (a.k.a. "Bloody Mary"), who tried in vain to reestablish an exclusive monopoly for Catholicism in England by stamping out all Protestant dissent.

Great Bible (1539)

Only 1,500 copies of "Matthew's Bible" were printed, and there were almost 9,000 parishes in England. Reprinting this edition on a large scale would risk the hostility of Tyndale's opponents. Thomas Cromwell solved the problem, with encouragement from archbishop Thomas Cranmer, by promoting a large-scale revision. The Bible itself would be a large folio. The published result was called the "Great Bible." King Henry VIII would be prominently displayed on the title page, as if he had championed the Bible in his native English all along.

Could the Bible now be used to promote royal interests?

As Lori Ann Ferrell says,

This image, then, like all elaborate title-page images from this period, should be read from the top down. To begin: Henry VIII sits enthroned at upper center, taking the place once occupied by the image of God in Miles Coverdale's Bible… Thus beatified, Henry hands copies of the Bible to churchmen at the reader's left and statesmen at the right. They in turn pass the books on to the lesser clerics and pious laypeople who populate the middle and bottom of the page.

opposite page
Title page of the Great Bible, 1539, with King Henry VIII at the top

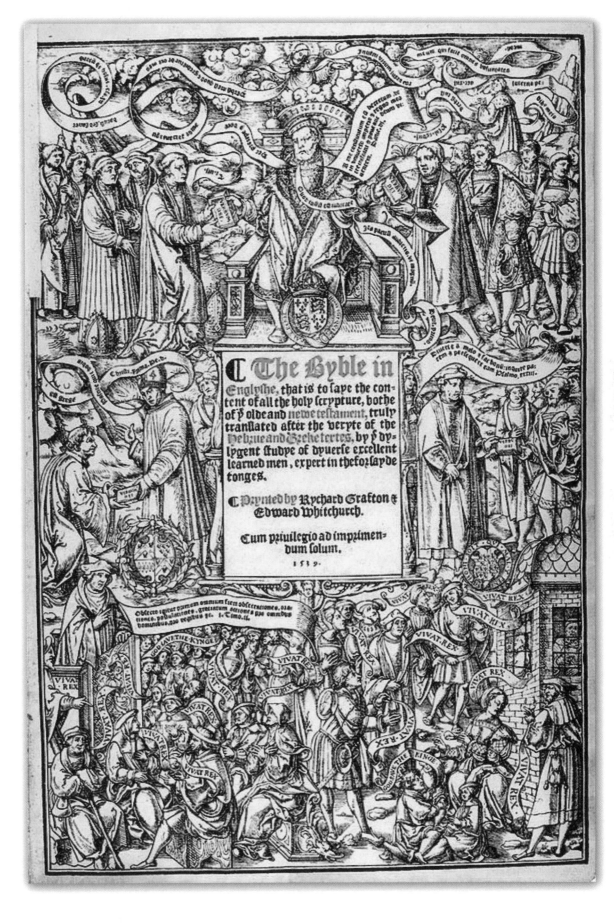

¶ The Byble in Englyshe, that is to saye the content of all the holy scrypture, bothe of ẙ olde and newe testament, truly translated after the veryte of the Hebrue and Greke textes, by ẙ dylygent studye of dyuerse excellent learned men, expert in the forsayde tonges.

¶ Prynted by Rychard Grafton & Edward Whitchurch.

Cum priuilegio ad imprimendum solum.

1539.

Even though the translation is still largely Tyndale's, the tribute to "the most noble and gracious Prince King Henry VIII," the inclusion of the Apocrypha and a red-letter holy day calendar, and the "Table of the Principle Matters Contained in the Bible" (favoring Anglican Church beliefs) reflect a decided shift into mainstream social acceptance.

The Bible was now a cultural phenomenon. King Henry VIII was vexed because the sacred words "were disputed, rimed, sung, and jangled in every ale-house." The king began to put fresh restrictions on the use of the Bible. After his death, the pendulum would swing all the way back to a radically repressive regime.

Geneva Bible (1560)

Queen Mary temporarily restored the Church of England to Roman Catholicism. With renewed attempts to burn heretics, Protestants were driven into exile. The Geneva Bible was first published in 1560 and was smuggled from the Continent into England. Geneva was the center of John Calvin's reforms, and this Bible, intended for the common people, was full of Calvinistic notes. The multitude of helps, maps, and "notes on hard passages" made it the original *Bible for Dummies*, according to Lori Anne Ferrell. This version also took highly resonating shots at the sinful Old Testament kings. Jehoram, for example "was not regarded, but deposed for his wickedness and idolatry"—words not exactly popular to 16th century European monarchs!

John Foxe's *Acts and Monuments*, later abridged to Foxe's *Book of Martyrs*, would document cruel atrocities carried out against reformers who spoke out against the establishment. This is a fold-out page of Windsor Castle with executions of Protestants in the foreground.

In many respects, however, the Geneva Bible broke new ground. It was the first English version with numbered verses, the first with commentary notes, and the first with Roman typeface. This was the Bible of the Puritans, Pilgrims, and other dissenters.

But the Geneva Bible also was eventually printed in England in 1575 (New Testament) and 1576 (full Bible). Side notes still included a few blurbs offensive to powerful interests in England, but the Book of Common Prayer was added to the front, the Apocrypha included between the Testaments, and the Anglican Psalter-Hymnal added at the end of the Book of Revelation. This Bible was the chief translation of the common people and persisted as such until 1640, long after the King James Version was published in 1611.

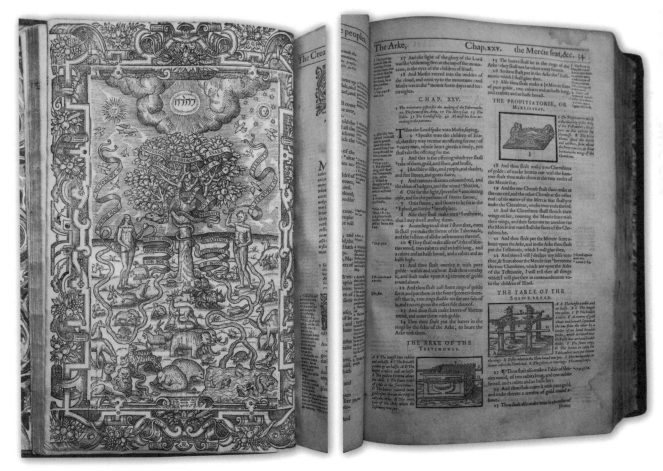

The Geneva Bible was crammed full of side notes, maps, charts, and illustrations.

The Bishops' Bible (1668)

As the Geneva Bibles were still streaming into England from continental Europe, the Archbishop of Canterbury, Matthew Parker, set out to produce a new version more favorable to Anglican high churchmen. The result was the *Bishops' Bible*, issued in the tenth year of Queen Elizabeth's reign. Although this version became the forerunner of the King James Version, it never really caught on, especially with the masses. Today, copies of the Bishops' Bibles still in existence are noted for their look of majesty and artistic grandeur. The translation itself is a bit stuffy and awkward. The lasting legacy of this edition is a version that is aesthetically pleasing to the eyes.

This rare 1572 lectern Bishops' Bible still has the original cover (leather over wood boards) and restored clasps.

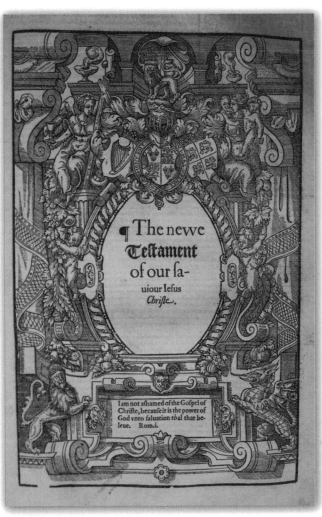

Internal contents, Bishops' Bible, with dedication to Queen Elizabeth I

The Douay-Rheims Version (1582)

Roman Catholic leaders, still somewhat in denial about the degree of earlier Bible suppression attempts, were late in the game with an English translation. The New Testament was issued in 1582 in Rheims, France by Catholic scholars associated with the University of Douai. The Old Testament was not issued in full until 1610. The side notes were strongly anti-Protestant. The preface, for example, claims that Protestants were guilty of "casting the holy to dogs and pearls to hogs." Hebrews 13:17 translates (or paraphrases), "Obey your prelates and be subject to them." Luke 3:3 says John the Baptist came "preaching the baptism of penance."

The Reuelation of Saint Iohn

the Diuine.

On the other hand, the very publication of this version was a tacit admission that Vatican City had lost the battle to keep the Bible out of the hands of the common people.

"The Sleeping Congregation" by William Hogarth. As the Bible became more accepted by mainstream society, the Anglican Church grew less interested.

opposite page
Chapter by chapter wood-cut scenes from the Book of Revelation, Bishops' Bible

The King James Version (1611)

In 1604 King James commissioned a Bible that is forever associated with his name. The king wanted something that did not have all the doctrinal notes of the Geneva Bible and was more favorable to the Anglican Church tradition. Translated by 47 scholars and printed by Robert Barker in 1611, the so-called "Authorized Version" became, in the words of Lori Anne Farrell, "the best-known, best-selling, most published, most widely-distributed... book in the English language."

John S. Tanner says, "The phrase 'Appointed to be read in Churches' announced a fundamental function of the King James Bible. It was intended to be read... aloud, in church... Tyndale's New Testament, by contrast, was written for individuals reading to themselves 'round the table, in the parlour, under the hedges, [or] in the fields,' not for congregations 'obediently sitting in rows in stone churches' being read to by the parson or 'squire at the lectern' (David Daniell). The Tyndale New Testament was small enough to fit comfortably in the hand. Not so the first edition King James Version. It was a church Bible."

opposite page
King James Version, 1611, title page

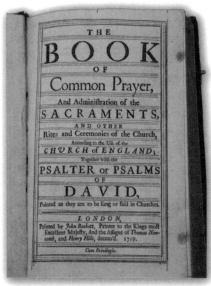  

Dissenters, Separatists, and Puritans objected that the "Book of Common Prayer" was becoming more important to many mainstream Anglicans than the Bible itself. The little "Bible" pictured in the two left photos is actually a red-ruled "Book of Common Prayer" owned by a young (teenage?) lady. On the right is a first-edition Cambridge Bible, KJV (1629), and the cover reflects the first section: "The Book of Common Prayer"!

The KJV, as this edition is often called, is not that of the 1611 version, but rather an edition extensively revised in 1769 for the Oxford University Press. The old spellings were modernized, but to modern ears, much of the old English persists (i.e. "thee," "thou art," "ye," "cometh," etc.).

Questions

1. The eventual acceptance of an English Bible was a double-edged sword. It was finally legal to own a copy, without fear of persecution or death, yet mainstream acceptance brought new dangers of assimilation with the world. Why was this so? James 4:4

2. Gradually many Anglicans paid more attention to the Book of Common Prayer than to the Bible itself. Eventually, some stopped paying attention to the Bible altogether. Give some reasons why daily Bible reading is essential to a vibrant spiritual life. 2 Tim 3:16–17

3. Early copies of the English Bible versions mentioned in this lesson are regarded as historical curiosities, museum pieces, or ancient works of art to be put on display. How should we regard the Bible, and where does God ultimately want its contents stored? Ps 119:11; Jer 31:33

4. Even with cultural and packaging liabilities and other human imperfections, many people were still able to come to a knowledge of the truth through these early English translations. It is better to have a less-than-perfect human translation of the Bible than no Bible at all. Tyndale recognized this in his note "To the Reader" in his 1526 New Testament: "Count it a thing not having his full shape, but as it were born before his time, even as a thing begun rather than finished. In time to come (if God have appointed us thereunto) we will give it his full shape…" In what respects is each of us, as a child of God, also a "work in progress"? Phil. 1:6

5. For diligent students: Do a little research on one of the Bible versions in this chapter. What are some of its strengths and weaknesses as a published translation?

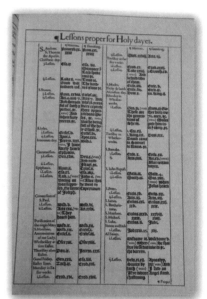

The original KJV Bibles contained a tribute to King James, a "holy day" calendar for Anglicans, the Apocrypha, and extensive genealogical tables. On the other hand, they (intentionally) lacked the extensive side notes of the Geneva Bible.

Helpful References

"Early Modern English Bible Translations," Wikipedia.org. https://rsc.byu.edu/archived/king-jamesbible-and-restoration/8-appointedbe-read-churches#_edn2

Donald L. Brake, *A Visual History of the English Bible: The Dramatic Story of the World's Best-Known Translation.* Grand Rapids, MI: Baker Books, 2011.

Melvyn Bragg, *The Book of Books: The Radical Impact of the King James Bible, 1611–2011.* London: Hodder & Stoughton, 2011.

David Daniell, *The Bible in English: Its History and Influence.* New Haven: Yale University Press, 2003.

Lori Anne Ferrell, *The Bible and the People.* New Haven: Yale University Press, 2008.

And lest one idolize the King James Version too much…

One of the KJV translators, Daniel Featley, published a book, *The Dippers dipt. Or the Anabaptists Duck'd and Plung'd Over Head and Eares* in 1645. Full of specious arguments defending infant baptism and the Anglican Church hierarchy, he attacks and parodies those who insisted on immersing adults who had been sprinkled as children. This was after a famous debate at Southwark between Doctor Featley and some representatives of Churches of Christ (later called "Baptists" in England). A page in the front caricatures all "anabaptists" who "rebaptize" the faithful…

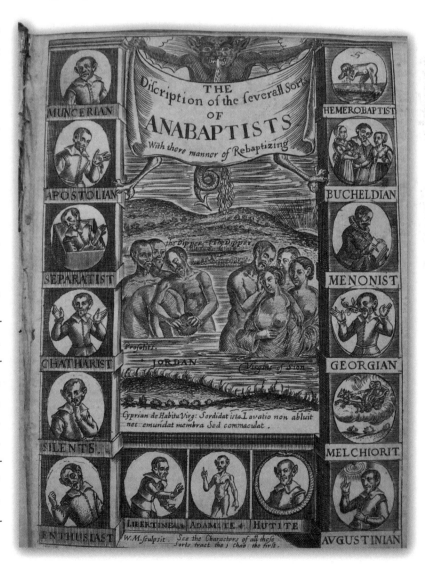

vnd wen gestlacht sie zerknyscht
dem haupt vnd du wirst went un
kuestutin Auch sprach got zu d
krauen Ich wird meru dein vttrw
vnd dem gepurd wirstu gepern in
smerttu dein kinder vnd vntter dei
mans gewalt wirstu sein vnd er
wirt uber dich herschen Aber zu
Adam sprach er Darumb an du
gehort hast die stym deins weibs vn
hast gessu von de holtz des ich dir v
poten hab an du es nit eut Ver-
flucht sei die erd in derm pau vn
werck In arbait wstu essu dauon
alltag deins lebens Sie wirt dir
gepern dörn vn distln vnd wirst
essu kreuter d erden In de swais dei
es angesichts wostu gespeist mit dem
em prot als lanng pis du widkumbst
in die erd wo d du genumen pist
mitub du pist asch vn wirst wid
werdn zu aschn Vn Ada hies de na
men seins weibs Eua durub an sie
war mut allr lebenden vn d her got
macht Ade vn seine weib eue peltzeu
töck vn leyts in an vnd sprach Nym
war Adam ist wordn als euer von
vns Erist willeut an gut vn pos
durub seht in an das er villeicht
lass sein haut vnd nem auch von
dem holtz des lebens vnd ess vn leb
ummer ewurklich

Vnd der herr got sant in aus dem
paradis der wolluft an er arbait-
tet die erd daraus er genummen ist
Er wirft aus Adam vnd setzt fur
an paradis der wolluft Cherubin
vnd ein feturin swert vnd pewei-
lich zu behuetten den weg zu dem
holtz der leben

Dann der als iiii cap
bekant sein weib Euam
die ward swanger vnd
gepur Cayn vn sprach
Ich hab besessen em menschn durch

LESSON 13
Where We Stand Now

As we bring these studies to a close, the situation at present can be summarized as "Better Information—Better Access—Better Reasons to Believe."

Better Information

We live in a post-Christian era in which anything "biblical" is attacked or dismissed without a fair hearing by many people. This is unfortunate because we have better information than we have ever had. In recent decades additional biblical manuscripts have been discovered, and stunning archaeological discoveries have provided a better framework for understanding the sacred text. Not only so, but an explosion of information is available to most people on the Internet.

I grew up on the King James Version and started preaching when personal computers and cell phones did not exist. How things have changed—and with advances in technology, the change will just accelerate! But having advantages in resources brings greater opportunities, as well as responsibilities.

Technology changes, but some things never change... like the value of reading the Good Book!

Painting from the 17th-century Dutch Golden Age, Pieter Janssens Elinga, "Woman Reading"

Better Access

The privilege of access is not limited to specialists. Amazing tools are available to virtually anybody. These include:

- Digital study tools on platforms such as Logos Bible Software of Biblesoft (PC Study Bible, Mac Study Bible, and Biblesoft App for the Cloud). Using computer-driven Bible software, I am able to find better information in a few minutes than what I found in hours (or even days) of painstaking research when I first started preaching.

- Helpful online resources. There are literally hundreds of user-friendly websites, jam-packed full of good information. A few are listed at the end of this chapter.

- Better translations than ever before. Wikipedia says, "As of October 2017 the full Bible has been translated into 670 languages, the New Testament alone into 1521 languages and Bible portions or stories into 1121 other languages. Thus at least some portion of the Bible has been translated into 3,312 languages."

There are reportedly over 300 translations of the Bible in English. A few of the better ones are the following:

- English Standard Version (ESV). 2001, latest revision 2016. With an "essentially literal" translation philosophy, produced by a top-notch team of scholars, and generally rendered into beautiful English, this is the author's personal favorite.

- New American Standard (NASB). 1971, updated 1995. Mostly faithful to the original text (as a literal rendering) yet highly readable in English, this is my second-favorite.

- New English Translation (NET). 2006, with a 2017 update. A version that promotes its online presence but is also available in print, this is a pretty good translation with extensive and insightful translators' notes.

- Christian Standard Bible (CSB). 2004. This version, produced by conservative scholars, seeks to achieve a balance between "formal equivalence" (literal word for word) and "dynamic or functional equivalence" (thought for thought). The goal was "to convey a sense of the original text with as much clarity as possible."

There are, of course, many other choices. The New King James Version (NKJV) is generally good, but isn't based on the best or oldest manuscripts. The New International Version (NIV) is still popular, especially in evangelical circles, but is somewhat less literal and at least slightly Calvinistic-leaning. I would advise avoiding The Living Bible (TLB), which is more of a paraphrase version than a formal translation.

Tyndale's 1536 New Testament. What would it have been like to read cases of conversion in English for the first time?

Better Reasons to Believe

The interplay that the average person can have with the sacred text has never been better. With the explosion of information, and the user-friendly availability of Bible-related materials on the Internet, the cases for God, Jesus Christ, and the Bible are as strong as ever. The key involves the degree of spiritual hunger (or lack thereof) motivating each person to embark on a search for truth. Consider carefully the words of our Savior:

- ► "You search the Scriptures because you think that in them you have eternal life; and it is they that bear witness about me" (John 5:39).

- ► "If anyone's will is to do God's will, he will know whether the teaching is from God or whether I am speaking on my own authority" (John 7:17).

- ► "I am the way, and the truth, and the life. No one comes to the Father except through me" (John 14:6).

- ► "Blessed are those who hunger and thirst for righteousness, for they shall be satisfied" (Matt 5:6).

- ► "No one can come to me unless the Father who sent me draws him. And I will raise him up on the last day. It is written in the Prophets, 'And they will all be taught by God.' Everyone who has heard and learned from the Father comes to me" (John 6:44–45).

Questions

1. No matter how powerful the transmission of a message, there has to be a "receiver" capable of picking it up, or else the communication is garbled and not heard. Unfortunately, "the god of this world has blinded the minds of the unbelievers, to keep them from seeing the light of the gospel of the glory of Christ, who is the image of God" (2 Cor 4:4). What attitudes on the receiving end must we have so that we may "see the light"?

2. Antagonistic attitudes toward the Bible are on the rise. Is this because of hard evidence against it or rather the false narratives of popular culture? Elaborate on your answer.

3. Someone says, "The King James Version has long been the best and most accurate translation of the Bible, and we should reject all these newer versions." How would you respond?

4. Someone else says, "The medieval Roman Catholic Church produced the Bible as we now have it." How would you respond?

5. What is the most important insight you have gained by going through all this material?

Helpful Online References

In addition to the books mentioned at the end of each chapter, I have also found the following websites to contain valuable and helpful information. Some of them contain really nice images of books and manuscripts:

https://www.wikipedia.org

Greek New Testament manuscripts, *http://www.csntm. org/Manuscripts.aspx*

Medieval manuscripts, *http://hcl.harvard.edu/libraries/ houghton/collections/early_manuscripts/bibliographies/ richardson.cfm*

Medieval manuscripts, *http://publications.newberry.org/ dig/rcp/introduction?path=index*

How We Got the Bible video, with Dr. Paul L. Maier, *https://www.youtube.com/watch?v=oo__F1Fiq1Q&t=1141s*

For general Bible research, *www.biblegateway.com* is a good place to start.

For excellent sources of antique Bibles and some good information about the history of ancient translations, the following websites are my go-to sources:

antiquebible.com

biblicalheritageexhibit.com

greatsite.com

Other Books by Mike Wilson

Evangelism Toolbox

Christians and Cancer: a Journey of Hope

Your First Steps: Learning to Walk with Jesus

Faith in Action: Studies in James

Biblical Secrets of Success: Wisdom from Proverbs

Inside Out: The New Covenant Written on the Heart

The Bible and Money: A Spiritual Guide to Financial Planning

Evangelism Training (soon to be published)

Lord's Supper Talks (forthcoming)

For more information, send an email to
mikewilson777@yahoo.com

GENERAL INDEX

SCRIPTURE INDEX

NOTES

NOTES

NOTES

NOTES